THE CHURCH

Life in the Renaissance
THE CHURCH

KATHRYN HINDS

BENCHMARK BOOKS

MARSHALL CAVENDISH
NEW YORK

To Maria

Grateful acknowledgment is made to Monica Chojnacka, Associate Professor of History, University of Georgia, for her generous assistance in reading the manuscript.

Sources for Quotations

Chapter 2: Luther to Pope Leo (p. 32) from Mitchell, *Rome in the High Renaissance*, p. 107. Chapter 3: Calvin on dancing (p. 42) from Rowse, *The Elizabethan Renaissance*, p. 248; Erasmus on destruction of images (p. 44) from Durant, *The Reformation*, pp. 410 and 411; "there are no organs . . ." (Bernardino Ochino, p. 45) from Durant, *The Reformation*, p. 476. Chapter 4: "The three vows . . ." (Johannes Trithemius, p. 50) from Durant, *The Reformation*, p. 20. Chapter 5: Arcangela Tarabotti on unwilling nuns (p. 58–59) from King, *Women of the Renaissance*, p. 90; Caritas Pirckheimer's memoir (p. 60) from King, *Women of the Renaissance*, pp. 99–100; "I saw him . . ." (p. 63) from Rabb, *Renaissance Lives*, p. 101; "In his hands . . ." (p. 63) from Rabb, *Renaissance Lives*, p. 103; "The greatest gift . . ." (p. 64) from Durant, *The Reformation*, p. 417; Luther on the mother of a family (p. 64) from Douglass, "Women and the Continental Reformation," p. 295; Katherine Zell's letter (p. 65) from King, *Women of the Renaissance*, p. 137. Chapter 6: "Any exercise . . ." (Philip Stubbes, p. 72) from Rowse, *The Elizabethan Renaissance*, p. 221; "When he is not tending . . ." (p. 74) from Ginzburg, *The Night Battles*, p. 120; wedding vow (p. 76) from Logan et al., *The Norton Anthology of English Literature*, p. 555. Chapter 7: "The Spanish Fleet . . ." (John Gerard, p. 80 from Time-Life Books, *What Life Was Like in the Realm of Elizabeth*, pp. 103–104; "They who at first . . ." (Hendrik Spieghel, pp. 83) from Murray, *Antwerp in the Age of Plantin and Brueghel*, p. 41; Montaigne quotes (p. 84) from Black, *Cultural Atlas of the Renaissance*, p. 179.

All biblical quotes are from the Holy Bible, Revised Standard Version.

All Shakespeare quotes are from William Shakespeare, *Complete Works, Compact Edition*, edited by Stanley Wells et al. (Oxford: Clarendon Press, 1988).

The recipe for hot cross buns (p. 70) is based on recipes from *The Joy of Cooking* by Irma S. Rombauer and Marion Rombauer Becker (Indianapolis: Bobbs-Merrill, 1975).

Benchmark Books
Marshall Cavendish
99 White Plains Road
Tarrytown, New York 10591-9001
www.marshallcavendish.com

Copyright © 2004 by Marshall Cavendish Corporation

Library of Congress Cataloging-in-Publication Data
Hinds, Kathryn, 1962-
The church / by Kathryn Hinds.
p. cm. — (Life in the Renaissance)
Summary: A description of the religious controversies of the Renaissance and Reformation with a focus on what life was like for ordinary people, both Catholic and Protestant.
Includes bibliographical references and index.
ISBN 0-7614-1679-X
1. Reformation—Juvenile literature. 2. Renaissance—Juvenile literature. 3. Europe—Religious life and customs. [1. Reformation. 2. Renaissance. 3. Church history. 4. Europe—Religious life and customs.]
I. Title. II. Series.

BR308.H56 2003
274'.05—dc21   2003008258

Art research by Rose Corbett Gordon, Mystic CT
Cover: Vatican Museums and Galleries/Bridgeman Art Library.
Page 1: Peter Willi/Bridgeman Art Library; 2:The Art Archive/Museo del Prado Madrid/Dagli Orti; 8: York City Art Gallery/Bridgeman Art Library; 11: Museo di San Marco dell'Angelico, Florence/Bridgeman Art Library; 13: Museo Poldi Pezzoli. Milan/Bridgeman Art Library; 15: The Art Archive/Musée Royale des Beaux Arts Antwerp/Album/Joseph Marti; 17: Ognissanti Church, Florence/Bridgeman Art Library; 18: Alinari/Art Resource, NY; 20: Art Resource, NY; 21: Private Collection/Bridgeman Art Library; 22: Palazzo Ducale, Urbino/Bridgeman Art Library; 25: Vatican Museums and Galleries/Bridgeman Art Library; 26: National Gallery, London/Bridgeman Art Library; 27: Index/Bridgeman Art Library; 29: The Art Archive/Palatine Library Parma/Dagli Orti; 31: Pierpont Morgan Library/Art Resource, NY; 33: Germanisches Nationalmuseum, Nuremberg/Bridgeman Art Library; 35: Museo Nazionale de Capodimonte, Naples/Art Resource, NY; 39: The Art Archive/Dagli Orti; 40: Museo di San Marco dell'Angelico,Florence/Bridgeman Art Library; 43: Art Resource, NY; 45: The Art Archive/University Library Geneva/Dagli Orti; 47: The Art Archive/Archaeological Museum Madrid/Dagli Orti; 49: Monte Oliveto Maggiore, Tuscany/Bridgeman Art Library; 51: The Art Archive/Santa Maria della Scala Hospital Siena/Dagli Orti; 53: Kunsthistorisches Museum, Vienna/Bridgeman Art Library; 56: Private Collection/Bridgeman Art Library; 59: Art Resource; 61: The Berger Collection at the Denver Art Museum/Bridgeman Art Library; 63: Corbis; 67: Corbis; 69: Art Resource, NY; 73: Bibliotheque de Protestantisme, Paris/Bridgeman Art Library; 75: The Art Archive/Museo del Prado Madrid/Dagli Orti; 79: The Stapleton Collection/Bridgeman Art Library; 82: The Art Archive /Musée du Louvre Paris/Dagli Orti; 85: Giraudon/Bridgeman Art Library.

Book design by Patrice Sheridan
Printed in China
1 3 5 6 4 2

cover: A scene from the court of Pope Sixtus IV in the fifteenth century.
half title page: A nun with prayer book and rosary, painted in the early fifteenth century.
title page: A bishop anoints children with holy oil to confirm them in the Catholic faith, in a painting by fifteenth-century artist Rogier van der Weyden.

CONTENTS

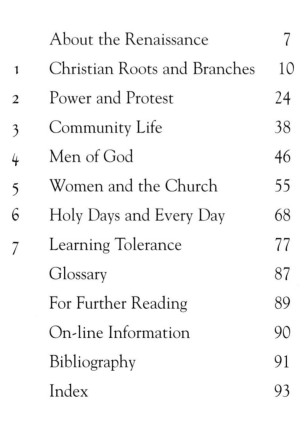

About the Renaissance   7

1   Christian Roots and Branches   10

2   Power and Protest   24

3   Community Life   38

4   Men of God   46

5   Women and the Church   55

6   Holy Days and Every Day   68

7   Learning Tolerance   77

Glossary   87

For Further Reading   89

On-line Information   90

Bibliography   91

Index   93

ABOUT THE RENAISSANCE

When we talk about the Renaissance, we generally mean the period of western European history from roughly 1400 to 1600. The Renaissance can also be understood as a cultural movement in which art, literature, music, philosophy, and education shared in certain trends and influences. This movement had its origins in fourteenth-century Florence, Italy. Here the great writer Francesco Petrarca, or Petrarch, promoted the idea of a rebirth of the literature and learning of ancient Greece and Rome—*renaissance* means "rebirth."

This notion gradually spread throughout Italy and much of the rest of western Europe. As it did, people also grew interested in giving new life to Greek and Roman styles of art and architecture. In the process of rediscovering ancient culture and adapting it to the times, Renaissance people began to create unique cultures of their own. Many Europeans developed a great love of beauty, art, and learning for their own sake.

Some Renaissance thinkers felt that they were living at the dawn of a magnificent new era, leaving behind a time they considered "the dark ages." They believed that they would not only revive the glories of the ancient world, but surpass them. This belief seemed to be confirmed as new artistic techniques, architectural styles, philosophies, and educational practices caught on all over Europe. Historians now realize, however, that the seeds of these magnificent achievements were already present in medieval Europe. But although the

Before the invention of the printing press, books were scarce. They had to be copied by hand. Often these manuscripts were beautifully written and decorated, like this book, which contains the words and music used in Catholic religious services.

Renaissance did not make a total break with the past, three momentous changes occurred during this period that definitely paved the way to the future.

First was the invention of movable type and the printing press. Two German goldsmiths, Johannes Gutenberg and Johann Fust, invented movable type in 1446–1448. Then, between 1450 and 1455 Gutenberg used the world's first printing press to produce the world's first printed book, the famous Gutenberg Bible. Before this, all books had been written out and produced entirely by hand. They were therefore expensive and fairly rare. Since most people could not afford to own books, most people did not learn how to read. With the printing press, books—and the ideas and stories contained in them—became much more widely available.

Second, the Renaissance was a period when Europeans made many voyages of exploration. Explorers originally sought new and better routes to Asia, the source of silk, spices, and other goods that brought high prices in European markets. In 1492 the Italian explorer Christopher Columbus landed on the island of Hispaniola in the Caribbean. At first it was thought that this land was part of Asia. By 1500 it was clear that Columbus had reached a continent whose existence had been previously unknown to most Europeans. It was a true turning point in world history.

The third great change for western Europe was the Protestant Reformation. During the Middle Ages, western Europe had been united by one Church, headquartered in the ancient Italian city of Rome. In 1517 a monk named Martin Luther nailed a list of protests to a German cathedral door. Luther hoped to reform the Catholic Church, to purify it and rid it of corrupt practices. Instead, his action sparked the beginning of a new religious movement. Now there were many conflicting ideas about what it meant to be a Christian.

Renaissance people had many of the same joys and sorrows, hopes and fears that we do. They were poised at the beginning of the modern age, but still their world was very different from ours. Forget about telephones, computers, cars, and televisions, and step back into a time when printed books were a wonderful new thing. Let the Renaissance come alive. . . .

One

CHRISTIAN ROOTS
AND BRANCHES

For more than a thousand years, one religion dominated western Europe: the form of Christianity that is generally known as Catholicism. The Catholic Church was a strong institution, providing order and stability to most of Europe after the fall of the Roman Empire in the late fifth century. From its headquarters in Rome, the Church was able to influence politics and society, as well as the religious beliefs of the people. From time to time, the Church's authority was challenged by small groups of people whose views on Christianity differed from official Catholic teachings. Nevertheless, for hundreds of years most Europeans were content to look to the Church to satisfy their spiritual needs.

In the middle of the fourteenth century this began to change. A terrible plague swept through Europe, in most areas wiping out one-third to one-half of the population. This disaster shook the faith of large num-

For all Renaissance Christians, the heart of their religion was faith in Jesus, who had overcome death and promised eternal life to all who believed in him. The first person to see Jesus after he rose from the dead was his follower Mary Magdalene, who encountered him in the garden outside his tomb.

bers of plague survivors. Many believed that the plague was a punishment for sin and that the Church had failed to help people overcome sin and its consequences. By the fifteenth century, large numbers of Europeans felt overwhelmed by a sense of human sinfulness, and they had a deep fear of going to hell. For numerous Christians, the Church's traditional teachings and ceremonies did little to help them feel assured of God's forgiveness.

At the same time, many people complained that the Church abused its power and paid more attention to worldly affairs than to matters of the spirit. By the early sixteenth century, a significant number of Europeans were longing for a purer form of Christianity, in which they could relate to God as individuals, without the aid of a Church that they now saw as hopelessly corrupt. They wanted a direct relationship with God, with no priests or saints standing in between. Only in this way, such people felt, could they be sure of salvation—the saving of their souls from eternal punishment for sin.

Inspired by such convictions, the Protestant Reformation began. It started out as a protest against certain practices of the Church. Gradually the protest evolved into an effort to reform the entire religious life of Europe. Protestantism had great appeal to many, largely because its services, hymns, prayers and, especially, the Bible were in the everyday language of the people—German, French, English—rather than Latin, which was used by the Catholic Church. For the first time, average people could read the Bible on their own. Many Europeans, however, remained passionately attached to the traditions of Catholicism. Each side was convinced that it was right. Religious differences resulted in widespread conflict—between husbands and wives, parents and children, rulers and subjects. Violence in the name of religion erupted again and again, ranging from riots to full-scale wars. To the people of the time, their very souls were at stake.

THE STORY OF JESUS

To understand what religious life was like for Renaissance people, we need to start with the beginnings of Christianity. Christianity was (and is) based on faith in one all-powerful, all-knowing God, present everywhere at every time. This same belief was (and is) also held by Jews and Muslims. Christianity, however, taught that the one God was revealed as three "persons," distinct from one another yet completely unified. The three-in-one, or Trinity, was made up of God the Father, God the Son, and God the Holy Spirit. The Son was Jesus Christ, and his life and teachings were the centerpoint of Christianity. His story is told in the Gospels, the first four books of the New Testament of the Bible.

Jesus was a Jew who lived in the kingdom of Judea (an area

The baby Jesus with his mother, Mary, by the great Florentine artist Sandro Botticelli

roughly equivalent to the modern nation of Israel) from around 4 B.C.E. to 30 C.E.* The Gospels relate that he was sent by God to save humanity from its sins. Jesus' mother was Mary, the wife of a carpenter named Joseph. The Bible describes Jesus' birth and one episode from his childhood, and then picks up his story at about the age of thirty. At this time, Jesus went to his cousin John for baptism, a ceremony in which John symbolically cleansed people of their past sins so that they could begin to live more righteous lives.

For the next three years, Jesus traveled throughout Judea, performing miracles, healing the sick, and teaching. Many of his lessons centered on the power of love: "You shall love your neighbor as yourself" (Matthew 22:39). Jesus also preached the importance of the Golden Rule: "Whatever you wish that men would do to you, do so to them" (Matthew 7:12). He taught that those who believed in him and followed his teachings would achieve salvation and have an eternal life in the presence of God. Jesus attracted a large number of followers, both women and men. Twelve of these followers, the disciples or apostles, were his most devoted students.

Judea was part of the Roman Empire, and some people feared that Jesus was trying to start a rebellion and make himself "King of the Jews." He was arrested and put on trial. Condemned to death by the Romans, he was crucified, or executed by being hung on a cross. Three days later, the Bible says, some of his women followers went to his tomb and found it empty. An angel told them that Jesus had been resurrected—he had risen from the dead. After this, Jesus appeared several times to his followers, promising forgiveness of sins and resurrection to all who believed in him. Then he ascended to heaven to rejoin God the Father.

*Many systems of dating have been used by different cultures throughout history. This series of books uses B.C.E. (Before Common Era) and C.E. (Common Era) instead of B.C. (Before Christ) and A.D. (Anno Domini) out of respect for the diversity of the world's peoples.

Jesus was crucified between two criminals on a hill outside Jerusalem known as Calvary or Golgotha, "the place of the skull." His mother and his disciple John stayed with him right up until his death.

THE CHURCH'S GROWTH

After the death of Jesus, his followers continued to spread his teachings. At first most Christians were Jews, who generally felt they were practicing a new form of Judaism. Soon non-Jews also began to embrace the Christian faith. Before long Christianity was an independent religion, practiced throughout the Roman Empire. Still, by the fourth century, only about 10 percent of western Europe's people were Christians, and Christianity had a much lower status than most other religions. But in 313, the Roman emperor Constantine decided to give Christianity equal rights and privileges with other religions. Most of the emperors who came after Constantine were Christians, and they continued to strengthen the Christian church. By the year 400 Christianity was the official religion of the empire.

Christianity also spread beyond the bounds of the Roman Empire. Over the course of several centuries, missionaries traveled to almost every part of Europe. They preached the new faith and established churches and monasteries. Many people were persuaded to convert to Christianity. When a ruler converted, he usually required all of his people to become Christians as well, whether they wanted to or not. In the countryside, though, people often continued many of their traditional practices alongside Christianity. For example, in parts of the British Isles people kept up the ancient practice of lighting bonfires and leaping over them on Midsummer's Eve, simply moving the celebration from the summer solstice (around June 21) to the Feast of Saint John (June 24).

Holy Helpers

The Church grew not only in size, but also in beliefs. As time went on, Catholics honored more and more saints. These were people who had led especially holy lives and, after death, were felt to be able to help humans

Saint Augustine of Hippo, by Sandro Botticelli. Augustine converted to Christianity in 387 and helped spread the religion in his native North Africa. He was also one of the early Church's most important writers and teachers.

Shakespeare and the Supernatural

"There are more things in heaven and earth . . . than are dreamt of in our philosophy," says the title character in William Shakespeare's great play *Hamlet*. Many Renaissance people agreed with him, believing in ghosts, fairies, witches, prophetic dreams, astrology, and various forms of magic. Religious authorities tried to discourage these beliefs, but the supernatural still kept a hold on people's imaginations. Shakespeare often portrayed such beliefs in his plays, as in the following selections.

Some people believe that this miniature painting, by Nicholas Hilliard, portrays Shakespeare at the age of twenty-four. The hand descending from a cloud hints at the role of the supernatural in the beliefs of many Renaissance people.

Witches Brew a Potion

Double, double, toil and trouble,
Fire burn, and cauldron bubble.
Fillet of a fenny snake,
In the cauldron boil and bake.
Eye of newt and toe of frog,
Wool of bat and tongue of dog,
Adder's fork and blind-worm's sting,
Lizard's leg and owl's wing,
For a charm of powerful trouble,
Like a hell-broth boil and bubble.

—*Macbeth*, Act 4, Sc. 1

A Ghost Speaks

I am thy father's spirit,

Doomed for a certain term to walk the night,

And for the day confined to fast in fires

Till the foul crimes done in my days of nature

Are burnt and purged away. But that I am forbid

To tell the secrets of my prison-house

I could a tale unfold whose lightest word

Would harrow up thy soul, freeze thy young blood,

Make thy two eyes like stars start from their spheres,

Thy knotty and combined locks to part,

And each particular hair to stand on end

Like quills upon the fretful porcupine.

But this eternal blazon must not be

To ears of flesh and blood. . . .

—Hamlet, Act 1, Sc. 5

An elflike being called the pwca has played an important part in Welsh folk beliefs for centuries. In Shakespeare's play A Midsummer Night's Dream, *the pwca became Puck, a mischievous member of the fairy kingdom and one of Shakespeare's most popular characters.*

with various aspects of life. The first and most important saint was Mary, the mother of Jesus. Her husband, Joseph, also became a much revered saint, and so did Jesus' disciples and other early followers. Many Christian missionaries became saints, and so did many of the Church's great teachers and visionaries. Such people were generally declared saints by the Church at some time after their death.

A great many legends grew up about the saints. Some of the most popular legends were about Mary or the disciples, filling in parts of their lives that were not described in the Bible—for example, Mary's childhood. Other legends were about early Christian martyrs, who died for their faith. There were also legends about saints who were not mentioned in the Bible or in any kind of historical records. These were often extremely popular saints, such as Saint Christopher, who was said to have carried the baby Jesus across a river on his shoulders. In addition, some saints' legends probably arose from stories about gods or goddesses who were worshipped before the coming of Christianity. For example, many scholars think that some beliefs about Saint Bridget of Ireland were descended from mythology about the ancient Irish goddess Brigit.

Saint Christopher, whose name means "Christ carrier," was said to be an immensely strong giant. People prayed to him for safety on their travels and for protection from sudden death.

Many saints were patrons, or special protectors, of particular countries, jobs, or groups of people. The missionary who brought Christianity to a country sometimes became that country's patron—Saint Patrick, the patron saint of Ireland, is a good example of this. Saint Christopher was the patron saint of travelers. Since Saint Joseph had been a carpenter, woodworkers of various kinds regarded him as their patron saint.

It was very common for people to pray to saints. God was felt to be far removed from human existence, but saints had once lived human lives. It was therefore easy to tell one's troubles to a saint, who could then carry the prayer to God. When seeking a saint's help, people often prayed before a picture or statue of the saint. If possible, they might pray at the saint's tomb or at a shrine dedicated to the saint. Some shrines housed relics—physical remains (usually bones) or objects associated with a saint. Holy relics had a great reputation for miraculous powers.

ACTS OF GRACE

The Catholic Church recognized seven sacraments. These were rituals or ceremonies that both demonstrated God's grace and bestowed it on those taking part in the sacrament. The most important of the sacraments was Holy Communion, which was modeled on the Last Supper, Jesus' final meal with his disciples. He had given them bread and wine, declaring that these were his body and blood, and bid them eat and drink in memory of him. At Communion the priest gave specially blessed wafers, called the Host, to worshippers, saying, *"Hoc est corpus Christi,"* which is Latin for "This is the body of Christ." Wine was also blessed in the name of Jesus, but only the priests drank it. The Church taught that during Communion, Christ was truly present in the Host and the blessed wine.

Holy Communion was offered at the daily worship service known as mass. The priests who conducted the service always participated in Holy

Jesus is baptized in the Jordan River by his cousin, John the Baptist. The sacrament of baptism recalled this important event for Christians.

Communion, but members of the congregation did so less frequently, even if they attended church every week or even every day. In order to receive Communion, a person was supposed to be cleansed of sin first. This was done in the sacrament of confession or penance, in which individuals confessed their sins to God through a priest. The priest then assigned a penance for the worshipper to perform in order to atone for the sins. The penance often took the form of saying a certain number of prayers. Some people confessed once a year or more, while others postponed confession until they were dying.

The other sacraments marked certain important events in a person's life. Soon after babies were born, they were welcomed into the church by the sacrament of baptism. During baptism the child was sprinkled with holy water and blessed in the name of God the Father, the Son, and the Holy Spirit. The parents and godparents pledged to raise the child to live according to the Church's teachings. The sacrament of confirmation, in which the child was anointed with holy oil, made the baptism complete. By the Renaissance, children were typically receiving confirmation around the age of seven.

Most people took part in the sacrament of matrimony, or marriage. But priests, monks, and nuns were not allowed to marry. The sacrament of holy orders was for men who dedicated their lives to serving the Church by joining the priesthood. Every Catholic, however, expected to receive the sacrament of extreme unction. This took place when a person thought to be close to death made a last confession to a priest. The priest forgave the sins and then anointed the person with holy oil in preparation for death.

Two

POWER AND PROTEST

Under the organization of the Catholic Church, all of western Europe was divided into parishes. *Parish* basically means "neighborhood"; a parish could be two or three small villages, a single village, or a section of a large village or town. Every parish had its own priest and its own church and cemetery. A number of parishes were grouped together to form a diocese, which was overseen by a bishop. An archbishop had charge of an archdiocese, a group of dioceses. At the head of the entire Church was the pope, who was also the bishop of Rome.

According to Catholic tradition, the first bishop of Rome was Saint Peter, one of Jesus' twelve apostles. The name *Peter* means "rock." Before Jesus died, he had said to Peter, "On this rock I will build my church. . . . I will give you the keys of the kingdom of heaven" (Matthew 16:18–19). The bishops of Rome came to be regarded as the successors of Saint Peter, and this was one reason for the pope's great authority.

Renaissance popes surrounded themselves with beauty and splendor, and their courts were often centers of art and learning. In this fresco, Pope Sixtus IV (enthroned on the right), appoints the noted scholar Platina (kneeling) as his palace librarian.

By the eleventh century, the pope was advised by a council called the College of Cardinals. All cardinals were appointed by the pope, who could name any Catholic male to the position. (Like the pope, cardinals held office for life.) It was common for popes to name relatives as cardinals and to grant cardinalships as a way of getting or repaying favors from powerful men. During the Middle Ages and Renaissance it was not necessary for a cardinal to be a priest. Sometimes it was not even necessary for him to be a grown man—the son of Lorenzo de' Medici, the unofficial ruler of Florence, became a cardinal at the age of thirteen. When a pope died, the College of Cardinals elected a new pope. From the 1300s on, all new popes were chosen from among the cardinals.

PRINCELY POPES

Medieval and Renaissance popes were actively involved with politics and other worldly affairs. Beginning in the 750s, the pope ruled Rome and the surrounding area, a region of central Italy known as the Papal States. Some popes were not above scheming or even going to war to increase this territory. For example, in the late fifteenth century the Republic of Venice was expanding south to the border of the Papal States. In 1508 Pope Julius II formed an alliance with France, Spain, and the Holy Roman Empire to destroy the Venetian state. In addition, the pope excommunicated Venice, decreeing that no one in the city might take part in any of the seven sacraments. (Most Renaissance people dreaded the punishment of excommunication, which they believed endangered their souls. The independent-minded Venetians, however, simply ignored the pope's order and continued to worship as usual.)

Pope Julius II, who personally went to war when necessary to maintain his power, was also an outstanding patron of the arts. This portrait of Julius is by Raphael, one of the Renaissance's greatest painters.

Many Renaissance popes cultivated a princely lifestyle. This was both a matter of personal taste and an effort to show the Church's power. One result was that the popes became enthusiastic patrons of the arts. Some of Italy's greatest artists and architects, among them Michelangelo and Raphael, worked on various papal projects in Rome. Both artists were involved in the construction of Saint Peter's basilica, the huge church at the heart of the papal court.

A few popes seriously abused their power for personal ends. The most notoriously corrupt pope was Alexander VI (pope from 1492 to 1503). He used his daughter Lucrezia to help him gain more power in Italy by marrying her first to one Italian ruler, and then dissolving her marriage so that she could marry another ruler. He also supported his son Cesare Borgia's conquests of several central Italian cities. Alexander and Cesare developed a murderous reputation for poisoning those who opposed them, including bishops, cardinals, members of Rome's leading families, and Lucrezia's second husband.

Some cardinals, too, seem to have cared very little for their own souls or anyone else's, but most were probably sincere in their religious beliefs. Nevertheless, cardinals tended to be much more worldly during the

Cardinals, like this elegant churchman portrayed by Raphael, were known by their red silk robes.

Neither Catholic nor Protestant

Although the Catholic Church held sway over western Europe, most Europeans east of Poland and Hungary belonged to the Eastern Orthodox Church. The Orthodox Church had split off from the Catholic Church in 1054, largely because the bishops of Greece and Asia Minor did not want to be subject to the pope. There were other disagreements, too, but even in the fifteenth century the two churches were holding meetings to try to overcome their differences and reunite. Few Eastern Orthodox Christians lived in western Europe during the Renaissance, except in Venice and its colonies. Venice, a thriving center of international business, also had many Muslim residents.

Much of eastern Europe during the Renaissance was ruled by the Ottoman Empire, a Muslim state. Some people in the Balkan Peninsula and elsewhere converted to Islam, but most remained Christian. Christianity was tolerated by the Ottoman government, although Christians did have to pay a special tax, and churches were not allowed to ring their bells. Until 1492 there was also a Muslim state in southern Spain, the kingdom of Granada. In that year, however, Granada was conquered by Spanish rulers Ferdinand and Isabella. Seven years later the royal couple decreed that all Muslims must either be baptized as Christians or leave the country.

In 1492 Ferdinand and Isabella had set down the same conditions for Spain's Jews. Not only in Spain, but in most of Europe, Jews were often viewed with suspicion and even hatred. Jewish customs and religious practices set them distinctly apart from the Christian majority. Jews did not accept the divinity of Jesus, and many Christians even blamed the Jewish people for the death of Jesus. There was also resentment against Jews because they often worked as moneylenders—a practice forbidden to Christians by the Church. (It was, however, one of the few ways in which Jews were legally allowed to earn a living in most European countries.)

The Jews of Spain were given four months to either be baptized or make their preparations for leaving. Around 50,000 Jews were baptized, but more than 100,000 emigrated. Some settled in Portugal, but four years later the Portuguese king also banished all Jews from his realm. In 1498 Nuremberg expelled its entire Jewish population, and other German cities soon did the same. (Jews had not been tolerated in England since the thirteenth century, when they were expelled. They were not allowed to return until the seventeenth century.)

Many banished Jews went to cities in central and eastern Europe, where they were able to build thriving communities. Jews who settled in the Ottoman Empire received the same religious tolerance as Christians there. A great many Jews moved to Venice and Rome. In fact, in Rome—the center of Catholicism—Jews lived in greater freedom and security than almost anywhere else in western Europe during the Renaissance. Unfortunately, even though their lives and property were protected by the pope, they constantly encountered prejudice in many forms. For all of the Renaissance's enlightened learning, it was an age when most people found it very difficult to understand or accept ways that were different from their own.

A Jewish couple read from a sacred text during their celebration of the Passover holiday.

Renaissance than now. Many patronized artists and writers, lived in luxuriously furnished palaces, and enjoyed hosting and attending lavish parties. Cardinals were often very wealthy men, and sometimes ambition for greater power tempted them into corruption. In 1518, for example, a group of cardinals plotted to kill Pope Leo X. Their plans were discovered; Leo forgave some of the cardinals after they made public confessions and paid him large fines, but the ringleaders were stripped of their rank and then executed.

The plots and abuses of power that went on in the papal court and among the cardinals upset many Christians. At lower levels of the Church hierarchy, too, there were practices that caused growing concern. Many bishops were appointed for personal or political reasons and never even visited their dioceses. There were also priests who seldom set foot in their parishes, but gave the care of their churches and congregations to others. Many priests were unqualified for their positions in the first place—for example, they were too young, or were not well educated in the Church's teachings. Priests of all ranks often had unofficial wives and fathered children, even though Church law prohibited priests from having relationships with women. Such inconsistencies fueled a growing dissatisfaction with the Church.

Tickets to Heaven?

One of the pope's spiritual powers was to grant indulgences. An indulgence was a kind of pardon for sins. Many people believed that an indulgence could reduce the time they would spend in purgatory, the place of suffering where the soul went after death to be purified before going to heaven.

Indulgences had been used in different ways over the course of several centuries. For example, a soldier who went on a Crusade was able to get an indulgence that accepted his fighting for the Church as a penance for any sins he had committed. Or an indulgence might be granted to a person

This illustration, from a German book published in 1521, shows the pope signing and selling indulgences.

who was given a difficult penance, such as going on a long pilgrimage, so that he or she could make a donation to the Church or charity instead. People who donated money in return for indulgences were, however, still expected to confess their sins in a prayerful spirit of remorse.

Receiving donations in exchange for indulgences became a way for the Church to raise funds. In 1515 Pope Leo X needed money to complete the building of Saint Peter's basilica. For this reason he authorized the archbishop of Mainz, Germany, to offer indulgences in return for contributions to the building fund. The archbishop's agents sold the indulgences and raised a large amount of money. But the agents did nothing to encourage buyers to have the proper spirit of penitence. Instead, they sold letters of indulgence that they said pardoned sins—even future sins—and eliminated time in purgatory. These certificate-like documents were sometimes mockingly called "tickets to heaven" by critics. The way the indulgences were sold made it sound to many as if the Church was saying that money was more important than prayer and that people could bribe God to let them into heaven.

The biggest critic of the German indulgence sale was the monk and university professor Martin Luther. In the fall of 1517 he wrote a letter of protest to the archbishop. Along with the letter he sent a list of criticisms of indulgences, hoping to encourage debate on the subject. According to tradition he also nailed this list, the Ninety-five Theses, to a church door, in his hometown of Wittenberg, that functioned as a kind of bulletin board for his university. Luther's protest soon snowballed into a movement that shook most of Europe.

NEW KINDS OF CHRISTIANS: THE PROTESTANTS

Thanks to the printing press, within a month the Ninety-five Theses were being read all over the Holy Roman Empire (centered in what are now Germany and Austria). Already disturbed by the other abuses in the Church, people debated not only the sale of indulgences but also the authority of the pope. Luther himself had not originally questioned the pope's authority, but before long he did reject it. In April 1520 he wrote to Pope Leo, "I must . . . acknowledge my total abhorrence [hatred] of . . . the Roman court, which neither you nor any man can deny is more corrupt than either Babylon or Sodom [cities described as centers of wickedness in the Bible], and, according to the best of my information, is sunk in the most deplorable and notorious impiety. . . . The fate of the court of Rome is decreed; the wrath of God is upon it."

Luther had other ideas that ran counter to the Church's teachings. In fact, he felt that the Church's teachings did not have any true spiritual authority, unless they were founded on what was written in the Bible. For Luther, scripture was the sole authority. Based on his reading of the New Testament, he came to believe that people could find favor with God only by having faith that Jesus had died for their sins. Good works—attending church, praying to saints, or giving to charity—could not earn God's grace.

As a result of these ideas, Luther recognized only two sacraments, baptism and communion. He also concluded that everyone who truly had

Martin Luther, painted by Lucas Cranach the Elder, a German artist who began the tradition of Protestant religious painting. Luther's gesture here seems to show that his heartfelt faith ultimately rests on the Bible.

faith in Jesus was equal before God. Therefore, there was no need for priests to act as mediators between individuals and God, and there was no special calling for monks and nuns to dedicate themselves to lives of prayer. Instead, every person was responsible for developing their own direct relationship with God, through simple faith in Jesus. To the many Renaissance people who were terrified of going to hell and felt powerless to win salvation, Luther's teachings offered new hope.

In January 1521 the Church excommunicated Luther. A few months later he had to attend a hearing before Holy Roman Emperor Charles V, who did not want religious controversies in his lands. Luther refused to change any of his ideas, and the emperor declared him an outlaw. Luther went into hiding for two years. During this time, he translated the New Testament from the official Latin version into German so that everyone would be able to read scripture for themselves. The ability of any Christian to read and interpret the Bible was to become one of Protestantism's key teachings.

Humanism and Reform

One of the great cultural movements of the Renaissance was humanism, which began as a program to reform higher education. For centuries, education had concentrated on logic and had been based largely on commentaries on the Bible and on a small selection of Greek and Roman works. Beginning in the late fourteenth century, more and more manuscripts of ancient literature and philosophy were becoming available in western Europe. These works—by Plato, Cicero, and others—inspired a number of scholars and teachers to encourage a course of study based on Greek and Roman models of education. The main subjects were those known as the humanities: grammar (or languages), literature, history, philosophy, and rhetoric (the art of persuasive writing and speaking). The Renaissance people who promoted and followed this program came to be known as humanists.

When the humanists studied Greek and Roman literature, they wanted to thoroughly understand the languages that the authors wrote in. They also wanted original sources, not commentaries or summaries, and they wanted the most accurate versions of these sources possible. This humanist concern with language, original sources, and accuracy soon came to influence religious studies. Scholars began to read the Bible and early Church records in a new, more critical way.

In 1440, humanist Lorenzo Valla examined a document known as the Donation of Constantine. It recorded a grant that the Roman emperor Constantine made to the pope, giving him and his successors rule over Italy as well as spiritual authority. Much of the popes' power came from people's acceptance of this document. Valla, however, was able to show that words used in the document could not have been in use during the time of Constantine—the Donation was a fake, produced in the eighth century. Valla's essay about his discovery was not printed until 1517, when German author Ulrich von Hutten came across it and had it published in Germany. In 1520 Martin Luther read this edition of Valla's work. The knowledge that the Donation of Constantine was a fraud helped Luther make up his mind to reject the pope's authority.

Some humanists used their new literary skills to study the Bible. In 1500 the Dutch scholar Erasmus decided to study the original version of the New Testament, which had been written in Greek. As he examined the Greek text, he realized that the Church's official Latin version of the New Testament was full of mistranslations and other mistakes. Erasmus spent several years making a new Latin translation. In 1516 he was finally able to publish this work, which included the Greek text along with his translation. At the same time, he also published a book of notes and comments on the New Testament. With these publications, Erasmus opened a new era of biblical studies. Moreover, he paved the way for the Reformers who would soon be publishing the Bible in German, French, English, and other languages, making the words and teachings of Jesus directly available to more people than ever before.

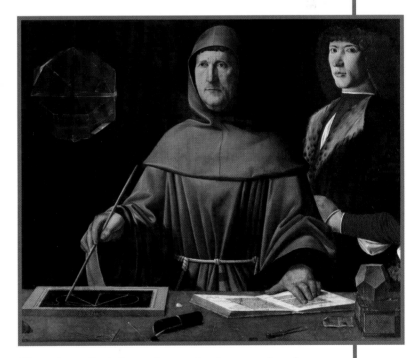

Humanist studies influenced many churchmen, such as the monk and mathematician Luca Pacioli, who studied and built on the works of ancient mathematicians.

Another important Protestant idea was predestination, which Luther first wrote about in 1525. According to this teaching, whether or not a person would achieve salvation was predestined from birth. In other words, since God knew everything about every person, from the beginning to the end of time, he already knew who was saved from sin and who was not. And since God was all-powerful, he alone was the cause of all human actions. Therefore, human beings had no free will to choose whether they would sin or not, and there was nothing that people could do to guarantee that they would go to heaven. Christians, said Luther and those who followed him, must simply have faith in Jesus and trust in God's grace and mercy.

Spreading the Reform

Luther wrote many pamphlets, books, and letters, which were printed and distributed widely. He also composed popular folksong-like hymns that expressed his faith. While the Church used Latin for all of its writings, Luther used German. The combination of printing and the everyday language of the common people quickly carried Luther's ideas throughout Germany, Austria, and Switzerland.

Among those who embraced Luther's reform were a number of German territorial rulers and independent city governments. In addition to the personal appeal of Protestant beliefs, political and financial considerations were also at work. Many German governments were glad to be free of the pope's authority, which they felt undermined their own power. Breaking away from the Catholic Church also allowed rulers to make great profits by taking over Church property—the Duke of Württemberg, for example, doubled his income in this way.

It wasn't long before Protestantism was making waves outside Germany. In Switzerland an influential priest and scholar named Ulrich

Zwingli spread many of Luther's teachings and gave his own version of others. Like Luther, Zwingli rejected the Catholic belief that Jesus was actually present in the bread and wine of Communion. Luther believed that Jesus was still present in spirit. For Zwingli, on the other hand, taking part in Communion was simply a way to remember and express thanks for the sacrifice Jesus had made for humanity. This symbolic view of Communion was taken up by many Protestants who came after Zwingli.

In the 1520s and 1530s, the kings of Sweden and Denmark embraced the Reformation. Lutheranism became the official religion throughout Scandinavia. In 1534 the English king Henry VIII also rejected the authority of the pope, for personal and political reasons. He established the Church of England, with himself at its head. Although Henry disbanded monasteries and confiscated their property, in many ways the Church of England stayed close to Catholicism.

At about the same time, the Frenchman Jean (or John) Calvin was developing another form of Protestantism. He took Luther's ideas about predestination and developed them further, giving predestination a central place in his teachings. For Calvin, everyone who had faith in Christ did so because God had already chosen them to be saved. Believers could therefore feel comforted in knowing that they were predestined for heaven.

Calvin's ideas became very influential among Protestants in France and the Netherlands, although both areas remained under Catholic rule. Some English Protestants, known as Puritans, wanted the English church to follow along the lines taught by Calvin. A Calvinist form of Protestantism did become Scotland's official religion in 1560. With this, over half of Europe had left the Catholic Church.

Three

COMMUNITY LIFE

In Renaissance Europe, there were several kinds of religious communities. Catholicism alone offered a range of options for involvement in religious life. The average person could simply attend church, listening to the priests chant the mass and joining in on the prayers. A very devout person might decide to join a monastery, a community of men or women who spent most of their time in prayer or good works. Protestantism, on the other hand, did away with monasteries. There was no role for monks or nuns to play in the new belief system.

A PLACE APART

A monastery was supposed to be a place where the cares of the world were put aside so that the residents could devote themselves completely to God. Some monasteries were in the countryside or in lonely places such as forests

The founder of the Dominican Order of monks and nuns was Saint Dominic, shown here in a fresco from a Dominican monastery in Florence. The artist was Fra Angelico, who was also a Dominican monk.

or islands. Other religious communities were on the outskirts or even in the middle of cities. Although monasteries were largely self-contained, monks and nuns were not always completely cut off from society—there was usually some interaction with the surrounding community.

The center of a monastery was its cloister, a square or rectangular covered walkway around a garden or open area. Many cloisters were enclosed, with glass windows looking out on the garden. Monks and nuns might spend hours each day in such a cloister, which often had alcoves where they could sit to read, pray, or meditate. From the cloister, monks and nuns could get to the other important monastery rooms and buildings, including the monastery's church. There was also a chapter house, the business center of the monastery. The refectory was the monastery's dining hall.

Fra Angelico's most famous painting, set in a cloister, shows the angel Gabriel telling Mary that she would be the mother of Jesus. The fresco adorned a wall near the dormitory in Fra Angelico's monastery.

Sleeping quarters were in a dormitory. This was usually a corridor or large room divided into small cells, each containing little more than a bed. A "night stair" often led from the dormitory directly to the church so that the residents could easily get to nighttime church services.

Large monasteries might have many other buildings besides those around the cloister. There could be workshops for different crafts, stables for horses, barns, a mill for grinding grain, and guesthouses. Guests entered the monastery through a gatehouse. This was also a place where poor people came to receive food, clothing, and other assistance from the monks or nuns.

Wealthy religious communities frequently owned farms, forests, flocks of sheep, ships, and other property outside the monastery walls. These resources not only supported the monks or nuns and aided the neighboring poor, but also financed the creation of masterpieces of art and architecture. Protestants saw such wealth as proof that the Church placed too much emphasis on worldly things. Lands and riches, they thought, were more appropriate for rulers than religious communities. For this and other reasons, the Church's wealth was an irresistible temptation to many rulers who embraced Protestantism. Between 1536 and 1540, for example, Henry VIII dissolved all 708 of England's monasteries, using their property to help refill his bankrupt royal treasury. As a result, 6,521 monks and 1,560 nuns lost their homes and their way of life, and around 12,000 people who had depended on the monasteries for their jobs or for charity had to look for other means of support.

THE PARISH

For most Renaissance people, Catholic or Protestant, the center of their religious community was their local or parish church. The church was at the heart of village or neighborhood social life in a variety of other ways, too. It functioned as a kind of community center, a place where meetings and other gatherings could take place. City churches often had large open squares or plazas in front of them, where markets were held on different days of the week. In some areas, especially in the country, the churchyard was a favorite location for dances. Churchmen had complained about this for years, and Protestants who followed Calvin were even more upset about it. Calvin himself called dancing "the chief mischief of all mischiefs." Reformers and Catholic priests alike disapproved of the gossiping and flirting that often went on during church services. Many Protestant groups took strong measures to control this behavior, often by making men sit on one side of the church and women on the other.

Inside a Catholic Church

Most Catholic houses of worship were built according to a specific plan. The focal point of the church was the choir, or chancel. This was always in the east of the building. Here was the high altar, where priests conducted mass and offered Holy Communion. The altar was on a raised platform reached by three steps, which symbolized the Trinity. At the back of the altar there might be an altarpiece, a painting or carved panel showing episodes from the life of Jesus or the saints.

The choir was only for members of the clergy and often was separated from the main part of the church by a screen carved out of wood or stone. While the priests chanted the mass and other services, the congregation listened from the nave. This was the central section of the church. At the head of the nave, just in front of the choir screen and to the congregation's left, there was a pulpit, a kind of platform raised up high. A priest stood here when he preached a sermon. Most churchgoers had to stand to listen, unless they brought benches or stools from home—there were generally seats only for members of the clergy and for the most prominent people in the congregation.

Catholic churches were decorated as beautifully as their communities could afford, often with precious objects that had been handed down for generations. There might be golden candlesticks, stained-glass windows, ornate wood carvings, and beautiful paintings and statues of Jesus and various saints. On the other hand, in rural villages the church was often a small, plainly decorated building. Sometimes the choir alone had a stone floor, the rest of the building having a floor of packed earth. But there were still beautiful and meaningful objects used in worship, such as the chalice to hold the Communion wine.

Inside a Protestant Church

At the beginning of the Reformation, there were no churches built specifically for Protestant worship. Protestants simply took over the existing church buildings. This was sometimes a violent process, especially in cities, where the Reformation movement was usually stronger than in the countryside. Many Reformers, believing that devotion to saints was un-Christian and kept people from relating directly to God, despised the paintings and statues of saints in Catholic churches. Some Protestants felt that any decoration at all in church distracted worshippers from God's word. There were even those who wanted to rid the churches of organs and other musical instruments, which were thought to be too worldly. On several occasions Protestant mobs fired up by these beliefs stormed churches and monasteries, smashing stained-glass windows, hammering statues to pieces, hacking up wood carvings, and in general destroying every religious image they came upon by any means possible.

The great Christian humanist Erasmus witnessed religious riots in Basel, Switzerland, in 1524 and 1529. He wrote that the rioters were "like men possessed, with anger and rage painted on their faces," and sadly mourned the loss of so much precious and beautiful artwork: "Not a statue was left either in the churches, or the vestibules, or the porches, or the monasteries. The frescoes were obliterated by means of a coating of lime. Whatever would burn was thrown into the fire, and the rest was pounded into fragments. Nothing was spared for love or money."

Aside from their decorations, church buildings had to be adapted in other ways to suit Protestant needs. Catholic worship services did not always include sermons, but Protestant ones did. To stress the importance of sermons and Bible readings, Protestants moved the pulpit into the nave, much closer to the congregation. Calvinists favored a simple wooden pulpit raised only a few steps high. Altars were replaced by communion tables, often set in front of the pulpit. In some churches, the clergy and the congregation's elected elders sat at the communion table to lead the service.

Protestants generally stood up to pray and sat down to listen to the sermon and Bible readings. To emphasize the belief that the clergy and congregation were spiritually equal before God, seating was provided for everyone. In many places, though, noble or wealthy churchgoers still had their

An early Protestant church, known as the Temple of Paradise, in Lyons, France

own family pews, located closest to the front of the church.

Martin Luther did not object to artwork in churches, so long as it expressed proper Lutheran beliefs. Many English churches, especially those far from London—the center of government and the Reform movement—were able to keep much of their Catholic decoration. But Calvinists preferred plain churches and simple worship services. An Italian Calvinist who moved to Geneva was full of praise for the simplicity of religious life in that city: ". . . there are no organs here, no voice of bells, no showy songs, no burning candles or lamps, no relics, pictures, statues, canopies, or splendid robes, no farces or cold ceremonies. The churches are quite free from idolatry."

four

MEN OF GOD

In the Catholic Church, there were two types of clergymen. The secular clergy were parish priests, bishops, cathedral officials, and the like. These men were out in the world (*secula* in Latin), interacting with ordinary people on a day-to-day basis. The regular clergy were those who lived according to a set of guidelines called a rule (*regula* in Latin), mainly monks. Their relationship to the everyday world varied depending on the requirements of their rule.

"IN THE WORLD BUT NOT OF IT"

A priest was empowered to offer Holy Communion, to preach, to bless, and to forgive sins. He could administer all the sacraments except confirmation and holy orders. If he was a parish priest, his main duty was to use these powers to care for the souls of the people of his parish. Someday, through

Catholic clergymen were set apart from their congregations in many ways, including a special haircut called a tonsure.

hard work and good fortune, he might become a bishop. Then he would be able to administer all the sacraments, and would supervise the priests in his diocese. Many Renaissance bishops were also powerful landowners and even territorial rulers—the German city-state of Cologne, for example, was ruled by its bishop.

A man was supposed to be at least twenty-five years old to take holy orders, the sacrament that made him a priest. During much of the Renaissance, however, exceptions were made to this rule for personal or political reasons. For example, Pope Alexander VI made his son Cesare Borgia an archbishop (a very high-ranking priest) at about the age of seventeen.

In theory, many years of study and devotion were necessary to prepare for the priesthood. In reality, this was not always possible. There were many priests who were very learned and devout. But there were also a great number, especially in the countryside, who had little opportunity to learn much Latin (the Church's official language) or to master the Church's teachings. Nevertheless, uneducated country priests were frequently loved and respected by their parishes—they must have had admirable qualities that made up for lack of learning.

Although the secular clergy lived and worked among ordinary people, they were set off from them in important ways. The visible sign of the clergy's dedication to religion was the tonsure, a haircut that left the top of the head bald. Clergymen also had special privileges. They were not required to serve in the military or to pay taxes. If accused of crimes, they could only be tried by the Church's courts.

Since 1074, priests had been forbidden to marry, because all their time and energy were supposed to be devoted to God. The ban on marriage was also another means of marking the unique role of priests, of making them different from other people. A great many priests, though—including high-ranking ones—did live with women and have children. Parishes often accepted this without any problem, even giving a priest's unofficial wife a place of honor at local festivals.

LIVING BY THE RULE

Almost from the beginnings of Christianity, there had been people who wanted to withdraw from the world and turn all their attention to God. Many such people gathered together in small communities devoted to the religious life; these were the first monasteries. Around the year 529, Saint Benedict wrote a book of rules to guide the monks of his Italian monastery. The Rule of Saint Benedict became the basis of monastery life for centuries to come.

All monks vowed themselves, for the rest of their lives, to poverty (they were not allowed to own any personal property), chastity (they could not marry or have relationships with women), and obedience (to the head of the monastery and to the Church's teachings). The rule gave further guidance to their lives. It covered everything from how religious services should be conducted to how much the monks should eat. These guidelines helped the monks to think of God and the monastery community before themselves.

In keeping with their vow of poverty, monks often dressed in simple brown woolen robes. The Rule of Saint Benedict said, "Let the monks not worry about the color or the texture of all these things, but let them be such as can be bought more cheaply."

Falling from Grace

Many monks had extreme difficulty living up to the high standards of behavior demanded by their monastery's rule. A great many monks, of course, remained true to their vows and performed their religious duties faithfully. Even corrupt monks didn't necessarily behave any worse than other European men of the time—but people expected more from monks. Here is the complaint of a German Church official, from around 1490:

> *The three vows of religion . . . are as little heeded by these men as if they had never promised to keep them. . . . The whole day is spent in filthy talk; their whole time is given to play and gluttony. . . . In open possession of private property . . . each dwells in his own private lodging. . . . They neither fear nor love God; they have no thought of the life to come, preferring their fleshly lusts to the needs of the soul. . . . They scorn the vow of poverty, know not that of chastity, revile that of obedience. . . . The smoke of their filth ascends all around.*

By the Renaissance, there were a number of different monastic orders. Each had its own rule, altering Saint Benedict's guidelines as needed to reflect the order's specific goals. For example, the Augustinian Order (which Martin Luther belonged to) was focused on good works, such as running hospitals, helping the poor, and teaching in schools and universities. The Dominican Order's special concerns were to improve people's morals and to make certain that people's beliefs were in line with official Church teachings. Dominicans were often highly educated, with a thorough knowledge of the Church's history, laws, and beliefs, so that they could effective-

Monks help doctors treat the sick in a fifteenth-century Italian hospital.

ly preach and teach these beliefs. Some of the Reformation's strongest opponents were members of the Dominican Order.

New orders were established in the wake of the Reformation, as the Catholic Church took various measures to reform itself from within. The most influential of these new groups was the Society of Jesus, or Jesuits. Members of this order, founded in 1540 by Ignatius Loyola, took the three traditional monks' vows and added a fourth: to serve the pope, without hesitation doing whatever he commanded for the sake of spreading the faith. The Society of Jesus focused its efforts on missionary work and education. In its first twenty-five years alone, the Society established 100 colleges and 130 monasteries. Jesuit teaching and preaching swayed Poland, most of Hungary, and parts of Germany away from Protestantism and back to Catholicism. The Society sent numerous missionaries to non-European countries, including India and Japan. Along with members of the Franciscan Order, Jesuits also played a major role as missionaries in Spain's New World colonies.

From Soldier to Saint

Ignatius Loyola, the founder of the Society of Jesus, was born into a noble family in northern Spain in 1491. As a boy he received little education, but he did love to read, especially popular tales of knights, love, and adventure. He grew up to become a soldier. When he was thirty years old, he was severely wounded in battle. At home in his family's castle, he had a long recovery and couldn't do much except read. The only two books in the castle were a life of Jesus and a collection of stories about the saints. At first Loyola was bored with these. But as he reread them, he became impressed with the heroic things the saints did for the sake of their faith. He vowed that once he recovered, he would spend the rest of his life as a soldier for Jesus and Mary.

At first Loyola thought he would go to Jerusalem and fight to take the holy city from its Turkish Muslim rulers. On his way to the port of Barcelona, where he hoped to get a ship for the East, he realized that the saints he admired fought with no weapon but their faith. Stopping at a Benedictine monastery, he left his sword at an altar dedicated to Mary, made vows of poverty and chastity, and received Communion. He then lived in a cave for ten months. He spent this time praying, doing penance for his past sins, and meditating on the life of Jesus. Sometimes he had visions of Jesus, Mary, and the Trinity. His meditations and visions led to the composition of his influential book *The Spiritual Exercises*, which continues to inspire Catholics throughout the world today.

After his months of prayer and meditation in the cave, Loyola resumed his journey to Jerusalem. He reached the holy city in the summer of 1523, intending to convert the Muslims to Christianity. For the sake of keeping the peace, he was persuaded to give up this idea and return to Spain. At the age of thirty-three, he decided to go back to grammar school so that he could learn Latin. He then went to college in Paris, to study for the priesthood. In 1534 he, his two roommates, and seven other men formed the Company of Jesus. They set off on foot

for Venice, where they hoped to get a ship for the Holy Land. This proved impossible, for Venice was at war with the Turks. Loyola and his followers decided instead to go to Rome and offer themselves to serve the pope. In 1540 Pope Paul III gave his approval to Loyola to found the Society of Jesus. Loyola worked tirelessly for the Society until his death in 1556. In 1622 the Church declared him a saint.

Saint Ignatius Loyola receiving a vision during Mass, painted by Peter Paul Rubens

PROTESTANT MINISTERS

One of Martin Luther's most important ideas was "the priesthood of all believers." According to this, no one needed a priest or anyone else to help them communicate with God—each person could and should pray and confess to God directly. Most Protestant churches did away with priests. Instead they had clergymen who were generally called ministers or pastors. *Minister* is from the Latin word that means "to serve," for these men were regarded as servants of God. *Pastor* comes from the Latin for "shepherd." Like a shepherd guarding sheep, a church's pastor was supposed to guide and protect his congregation.

Clergymen in the Church of England continued to be called priests, but they were not set apart from the rest of society like Catholic priests were. The most obvious sign of this was that priests in the Church of England, like all other Protestant clergymen, were both allowed and encouraged to get married.

One of a Protestant minister's most important jobs was to preach sermons. In his sermons, the minister was supposed to help the congregation understand the Bible and how it applied to their own lives. To be a good preacher, the minister had to have a thorough understanding of scripture and excellent writing and public-speaking skills. This required a particular kind of education. In many areas that embraced Protestantism, new schools to educate ministers quickly sprang up. For example, as soon as the leaders of Nuremberg, Germany, decided to make their city-state Lutheran, in 1525, they set up a school to train ministers. They brought in Philipp Melanchthon, one of Luther's closest associates, to plan the course of study.

Education was, in fact, one of the Reformation's greatest gifts to Europe. Most Reformers taught that everyone should be able to read the Bible for themselves. For this reason, Protestant communities generally did their utmost to make sure that every man, woman, and child learned to read.

five

WOMEN AND THE CHURCH

In Renaissance Europe there were many negative opinions about women. Although peasant women worked in the fields alongside men, and city women worked at almost every trade that men did, women were still thought of as weaker and less intelligent than men. Most authorities believed that women had to have the protection and guidance of men, and many laws reflected this. The inferiority of women was one subject on which most Catholics and Protestants agreed.

BRIDES OF CHRIST

In the early years of Christianity, women played an active part in spreading and supporting the new faith. The Catholic Church continued to give women roles in religion. Women could not join the secular clergy, but they

Two views of a Catholic lady holding a rosary, a string of beads used to help with concentration during prayers. The main prayer said with the rosary was addressed to Mary, the model of Christian womanhood.

could join monasteries and become nuns. As nuns, they made the same life-long vows of poverty, chastity, and obedience that monks did. A nun's vows were sealed by a ring that she wore to show that she had turned away from marriage and the world and was wedded to Christ.

Even so, nuns faced many of the same prejudices and restrictions as other women. The Church taught that women were naturally more sinful than men, and that women distracted men from religion. Women were forbidden to preach, to serve as priests, or even to assist priests during religious services. Women's monasteries were almost always supervised by men—the head of a men's monastery of the same order, or the bishop of the local diocese. Most importantly, every house of nuns had at least one male chaplain. This priest (or group of priests) conducted mass for the nuns, heard their confessions, blessed them, and received new nuns' vows. No woman was permitted to do any of these things.

Most women's monastic rules required the nuns to stay in the convent at all times, although some Renaissance convents had become fairly relaxed about this requirement. Many women thrived in the seclusion and discipline of a monastery, which offered them the opportunity to devote themselves to prayer and study. A monastery was often the only place where an intelligent woman was allowed to pursue an education, to write books, or to teach others.

Nuns often wrote of their happiness that they would not have to marry someone they might not love (most Renaissance marriages, especially in the upper classes, were arranged by the parents). They were also safe from the dangers of childbirth, which killed a great many women during this period. Renaissance nuns rarely did any kind of physical work. They were almost always from the upper classes; women from lower-class families also lived in convents, though not as full nuns, and did the cooking, cleaning, and so on. Prayer was the main occupation of both monks and nuns, who generally took part in eight or nine religious services a day. Some monastic orders offered women other kinds of fulfilling work, such as teaching the

An Unwilling Nun

The Renaissance saw an increase in complaints about nuns not living up to their vows and the simplicity of the monastic rules. There were indeed convents where nuns lived in luxury, ate gourmet meals, entertained visitors, spent their time playing the lute or doing elegant embroidery instead of praying, and left the monastery walls for picnics and other social outings. Part of the reason for such behavior was that a great many women were sent into convents against their will. Some were only nine years old, or even younger, when they began monastic life.

Parents placed girls in convents for various reasons, but the most common one was economic. Although a nun's family had to make a gift of money or property to the monastery she joined, this gift was much smaller than the dowry owed to her husband if she married. Many upper-class families, especially in Italy, were not willing or able to provide dowries for all their daughters. This was particularly true of parents who were trying to make sure their sons would have large inheritances. So, to save money, one or more daughters might be sent away to become nuns, often whether they wanted to or not. To such women, the convent was a prison.

Arcangela Tarabotti of Venice was placed in a monastery as a child and became a nun at the age of sixteen. She felt no calling to the religious life and hated it, but had no choice in the matter. Her anger was expressed in a book she wrote, *Simplicity Betrayed*, which was published two years after her death in 1652. Although Tarabotti lived slightly after the Renaissance, her words give voice to all the unwilling nuns of the earlier period:

> *It seems to me, when I see one of these unfortunate girls so betrayed by their own fathers, that I see that which happens to the little song bird,*

which in its pure simplicity, there between the leaves of the trees or along the banks of rivers, goes with sweet murmur and with gentle harmony . . . when there comes a sly net and it is caught and deprived of its dear liberty. In the same way these unhappy girls, born under an unfortunate star, pass the years of their innocent girlhood, and . . . please the ear and delight the soul of the base fathers who, deceitful, . . . think of nothing but to remove them from sight as soon as possible and so bury them alive in cloisters for the whole of their lives, bound with indissoluble knots.

Four German nuns praying during a church service

young—many convents included boarding schools for girls. A woman who truly felt a religious calling, in a community of like-minded women, could often find more support, more dignity, and more opportunities for self-expression in a monastery than anywhere else in Renaissance Europe.

Nuns and the Reformation

To sincere, dedicated nuns in many countries, the Reformation was a horrible blow. Most Protestant governments eventually closed down all monasteries, often turning monks and nuns out into the streets. This was especially hard on the nuns. As women, they had little freedom outside the convent and might have no way to earn a living. They generally had to marry or return to their parents' homes.

Many nuns fought the closing of their monasteries. Most were not successful, but a few were. Caritas Pirckheimer was head of a convent of about sixty women in Nuremberg, Germany. From one of the city's most influential families, she was highly educated and had contacts with notable scholars all over northern Europe. In her memoirs she described the struggle to save her monastery. For instance, one day three women, supported by a mob, came to take their daughters away from the convent: "The wives then bade the children come out with kind words, saying that if they did not do so willingly, they would pull them out forcibly. . . . The children cried that they did not want to leave the pious, holy convent. . . ."

The girls' protests did not win out—their families ended up taking them home by force. But Caritas Pirckheimer did not give up her fight to keep the convent open. The Nuremberg city council finally agreed. The monastery was forbidden to receive any new members, but all the nuns were allowed to remain in the religious life that they loved until their deaths.

SERVING GOD IN THE HOME

As they studied the Bible, Reformers noted that some of Jesus' disciples were married and that all the holy men of the Old Testament had wives and children. This helped convince Protestants that God regarded marriage as the ideal state for human beings. The Catholic Church had always taught that taking holy orders or monastic vows was the most righteous way of life. Now Reformers argued that rejecting marriage and making a vow of chastity was against the will of God. Luther himself, to set the example, married an ex-nun, Katherine von Bora, in 1525, and had six children with her. The

An English lady with her two sons. Like many mothers, both Catholic and Protestant, she has probably been her children's first teacher, helping them learn reading, writing, and basic prayers and religious beliefs.

Two Women of Spirit

Two of the most dynamic religious women of the sixteenth century were Angela Merici and Teresa of Avila. Both founded important new religious societies, within which they treated rich women and poor women as equals. Both were later declared saints. But each had a distinct vision of how a Catholic woman could best serve God. While Angela Merici wanted religious women to be active in the world, Teresa of Avila believed that nuns (and monks) could live more holy lives if they were completely cut off from the world.

Like a number of women since the thirteenth century, for many years Angela Merici followed a modified version of Saint Francis of Assisi's monastic rule while living in her own home. When she was in her fifties, she felt called to organize a group of young women who would be dedicated to prayer and charity. Merici's goal was for these women to actively serve people as Jesus' apostles had done. In 1535 she established the Company of Saint Ursula in Brescia, Italy.

The Ursulines, as they were called, made a lifelong vow of chastity as a loving sacrifice to God. During Merici's lifetime, they usually lived in their family homes. The Company helped members without families find jobs as live-in housekeepers or governesses in respectable homes. The Ursulines met together twice a month. The younger members were called daughters and received guidance from the mothers, older married women or widows. The mothers directed the group's activities, which included nursing, assisting the poor, instructing people in basic Catholic beliefs, and teaching in schools, especially girls' schools.

Ursuline communities were set up in France as well as in many parts of Italy. Church authorities, however, were always a little nervous about the Company's independence. After Angela Merici died in 1540, the Church pressured most of the Ursulines to live in convents and become a traditional monastic order. Only in Brescia and nearby Milan were they permitted to go on working in the world. Yet inside or outside the convent, the Ursulines continued to play an active and important role as educators.

When Teresa of Avila entered the religious life, she belonged to a convent in which the nuns were allowed to wear jewelry and had finely furnished suites of rooms. They were even permitted to leave to visit relatives. In the 1540s she began to receive visions of Jesus. As she later wrote, "I saw Him with the eyes of the soul more clearly than I could ever have seen Him with those of the body. . . ." Around 1560 she had an especially powerful religious experience. In a vision, an angel came to her: "In his hands I saw a long golden spear and at the end of the iron tip I seemed to see a point of fire. With this he seemed to pierce my heart several times. . . . When he drew it out . . . he left me completely afire with a great love of God."

Teresa came to feel that her visions were guiding her to leave her convent for a stricter life of poverty and prayer. In 1562 she founded her own monastery and a new order, the Discalced Carmelites. (*Discalced* means "shoeless"; the nuns wore rope sandals as a sign of humility.) Teresa's nuns had no furniture and were allowed no guests. They were so closed off from the world that they even covered their windows with cloth to block off any view of the outside. They supported themselves by spinning and sewing, leaving their finished work on a revolving disk built into the convent wall. Anyone from the outside could take what they wanted from the outer half of the disk and leave food or other donations in exchange. Teresa and her nuns soon became well known for their holiness. Within a few years Teresa was asked to help establish similar monasteries throughout Spain, not only for nuns but also for monks. Teresa worked tirelessly on this mission, overcoming many difficulties, until her death in 1582.

Saint Teresa of Avila at the age of sixty-one, with a dove representing the Holy Spirit. The Latin words above her head mean, "I will praise the Lord's mercy in song forever."

marriage was such a happy one that Luther once declared, "The greatest gift of God to man is a pious, kindly, God-fearing, home-loving wife." The Reformers, however, were still convinced that women were weaker and less intelligent than men. Their weakness, though, was made up for by their ability to bear children. In fact, the Reformers thought, giving birth was one of the noblest works that women could do for God.

All Protestant women were expected to marry, have children, help their husbands, and run a home. The Reformers considered this the ideal Christian life for a woman. As Luther wrote, "If a mother of a family wishes to please and serve God, let her not do what the papists [Catholics] are accustomed to doing: running to churches, fasting, counting prayers, etc. But let her care for the family, let her educate and teach her children, let her do her task in the kitchen . . . if she does these things in faith in the Son of God, and hopes that she pleases God on account of Christ, she is holy and blessed."

Protestant guidelines for marriage were based on the Bible. In the New Testament, husbands were instructed to love their wives, but wives were told to obey their husbands: "Wives, be subject to your husbands, as to the Lord. For the husband is the head of the wife as Christ is the head of the church. . . . As the church is subject to Christ, so let wives also be subject in everything to their husbands" (Ephesians 5: 22–24). While Catholic women relied on their priests for spiritual guidance, in Protestantism the husband, as head of the family, was in charge of his wife's spiritual life. He was expected to teach her and to keep her from sinning. He was also supposed to take care of her just as he cared for himself. In return, the wife should always be ready to help him in every area of life.

For many Protestant husbands and wives, their shared faith brought them close. They prayed and studied the Bible at home together, often with their children. A minister's wife might be able to participate in, or at least listen to, religious discussions between her husband and his students or friends. Protestant women also did charitable work for their congregations and communities. Many women thrived in this atmosphere and played their own role in spreading the Reform movement.

A Letter from a Minister's Wife

Katherine Zell's husband, Matthias, was a former priest. He became a Protestant pastor in Strasbourg, a German city within the Holy Roman Empire.* When Catholic authorities criticized Matthias for marrying, Katherine spoke out in a well-argued essay defending the right of ministers to marry. Being a pastor's wife allowed Katherine Zell to live a life that she found very fulfilling, as she wrote in a letter to the citizens of Strasbourg near the end of her life:

> *That I learned to understand and helped to acknowledge the Gospel I shall let God declare. That I married my pious husband and for this endured slander and lies, God knows. The work which I carried on both in the house and out is known both by those who already rest in God and those who are still living, how I helped to establish the Gospel, took in the exiled, comforted the homeless refugees, furthered the church, preaching and the schools, God will remember even if the world may forget or did not notice . . . I honored, cherished, and sheltered many great, learned men, with care, work, and expense . . . I listened to their conversation and their preaching, I read their books and their letters and they were glad to receive mine . . . and I must express how fond I was of all the old, great learned men and founders of the Church of Christ, how much I enjoyed listening to their talk of holy things and how my heart was joyful in these things.*

*Today Strasbourg is part of France, very close to the border with Germany.

Like men, women participated in the prayers and hymn-singing in Protestant churches. However, they could not preach or take any kind of leadership role, for the Bible said, "the women should keep silent in the churches. For they are not permitted to speak, but should be subordinate, as even the law says. If there is anything they desire to know, let them ask their husbands at home. For it is shameful for a woman to speak in church" (1 Corinthians 14:34–35). Women might sometimes give religious instruction to other women, though, and mothers were expected to help their children to be good Christians. In special circumstances (and outside of church), women might also preach to other women. For example, a group of Protestant women went to a Geneva convent several times to try to persuade the nuns to leave it (with little success).

WOMEN UNDER SUSPICION: THE WITCH HUNTS

Both Catholic and Protestant churches believed that women needed male guidance and supervision. The different branches of Renaissance Christianity generally agreed on something else: the existence of evil witches. Until the thirteenth century, the Church had taught that belief in witchcraft was an illusion caused by the devil. Gradually, though, influential churchmen accepted and spread the idea that there were witches who flew through the air to gatherings in the night, where they rejected Jesus and promised to serve the devil. They were said to cause storms, damage crops, harm livestock, ruin wine, kill babies, and the like.

After the invention of the printing press, books and pamphlets describing these witches were published, and a great many copies were sold. Fear of witchcraft grew, and governments set up procedures for putting suspected witches on trial. The accused were almost always tortured until they confessed. Condemned witches were executed, and their bodies were often burned at the stake—the usual punishment for heresy, a crime against religion.

Women with mental illness were in great danger of being accused as witches. In other cases, mental illness might be interpreted as demonic possession, and priests could be summoned to exorcise, or cast out, the demon, as in this scene.

From about the last part of the fifteenth century to the middle of the seventeenth century, thousands of witch hunts were carried on by government or religious officials. They were most common in the Holy Roman Empire, peaking in the 1500s and early 1600s. In all, around 110,000 Europeans were accused of witchcraft. About 60,000 of them were executed. (These numbers are low estimates—some sources give numbers as high as 1,500,000.)

An average of about 75 percent of the people accused of witchcraft were women—but in some areas, it was as high as 95 percent. We know of one German town where witch hunters accused all but two of the townswomen of witchcraft. Most commonly, throughout Europe, suspected witches were poor, uneducated women over the age of forty. They were often sharp-tongued or quarrelsome—or perhaps just too "uppity" for their neighbors. Midwives, who delivered babies and treated women's health problems, were frequently accused. So were other women healers—sometimes even when their cures worked. But when a witch hunt was under way, no woman was free from suspicion.

Six

HOLY DAYS AND EVERY DAY

Religion was woven into the lives of Renaissance Europeans in a variety of ways. It influenced the holidays they celebrated, the names they gave their children, the clothes they wore, the food they ate, the way they handled birth and death. Even people who did not have strong personal religious beliefs could not help being affected by the Catholicism or Protestantism of the time.

HOLY DAYS

During the Renaissance, all holidays had a religious significance. In Catholic areas, there were many holidays throughout the year. For example, the Italian city of Florence celebrated around forty feast days; Venice celebrated around ninety. These holy days included Christmas, Easter, and other days that honored events in the life of Jesus. There were also many

Singing was an important and much loved part of many church services, especially on holy days. This choir seems to be particularly enthusiastic.

holidays that commemorated the life of his mother, Mary. The other celebrations were devoted to various saints.

For all of these holy days, people got a full or half day off from work. The celebrations often included elaborate processions, or parades, in which beautiful statues of saints were carried through the streets. On some holidays there were plays in which Bible stories were acted out. Church services might include special music and prayers. Holidays were also times for dances, feasts, bonfires, fireworks, races, and performances by jugglers, magicians, and acrobats.

Hot Cross Buns: A Recipe for Easter and All Year 'Round

An Easter tradition in Renaissance England was baking hot cross buns. The cross of icing on top of each bun symbolized Jesus' death and resurrection. A variety of folk beliefs surrounded the buns, too. People kept Easter's hot cross buns long after the holiday was over, for it was said that they would never go moldy. Many people believed that the buns brought good luck and that they could cure diseases in people and in livestock. Sailors even carried hot cross buns with them on voyages as a protection against shipwrecks.

Whether you celebrate Easter or not, you can still experience a bit of Renaissance culture and enjoy delicious hot cross buns. To make them, you will need a bread or roll mix, such as Pillsbury's Hot Roll Mix, and any additional ingredients required for the mix, along with:

1/4 cup sugar
1/4 teaspoon cinnamon
1/8 teaspoon nutmeg
1/4 cup raisins

1/2 cup sifted confectioners' sugar
2 teaspoons hot milk
1/4 teaspoon vanilla extract

Mix the sugar, cinnamon, nutmeg, and raisins together. Add this mixture to the flour in the roll mix. Follow the directions on the roll mix box to make the dough for the buns. After the dough has risen the first time, shape it into 18 balls and arrange them on a greased cookie sheet. Cover the sheet with a clean dish towel and let the buns rise to about twice their original size. While they are rising, preheat your oven to 425°. Bake the buns until they are golden brown (about 20 minutes).

When the buns are cool, combine the confectioners' sugar, hot milk, and vanilla extract. Mix until smooth. Drizzle this glaze from a spoon to make an equal-armed cross on top of each bun. Let the glaze harden, then eat and enjoy!

Many Protestants objected to the nonreligious activities that took place on holy days. They also objected to certain of the holidays themselves. Most Protestants put much less importance on Mary than Catholics did, and almost no importance at all on other saints. Protestant communities therefore celebrated far fewer holidays. In England, for example, the number of recognized festivals was reduced from ninety-five before the Reformation to twenty-seven afterward. A number of Protestant groups celebrated only Christmas and Easter. Some of the strictest followers of Jean Calvin recognized Easter alone.

In cities with both Protestants and Catholics, holidays were sometimes a source of conflict. Protestants complained about Catholics not working on holidays. Catholics were insulted that Protestants did work. In some cities, Lutheran or Calvinist women would sit right by their windows to sew and spin so that Catholics passing by in religious processions would have to notice them. In one French city, on a couple of occasions, some Protestant women did their laundry on Catholic holidays, and Catholics threw the clothes into the river.

The Lord's Day

Both Catholics and Protestants celebrated Sunday as a holiday and a day off from work. In many places, such as England, the law required people to attend church every week and to take Communion a certain number of times a year. (And from 1570 into the 1590s, the law also demanded that Englishmen, except for nobles, wear woolen caps to church—part of a government plan to support the nation's wool industry.) After the worship service, or between morning and evening services, there was often time for fun and relaxation.

During the reign of Queen Elizabeth I, English country people enjoyed playing a rough form of football on Sunday afternoons. This kind of thing was fiercely criticized by Puritan writers and preachers: "Any exercise which withdraweth us from godliness, either upon the sabbath or any other day, is wicked and to be forbidden. . . . As concerning football-playing, I protest unto you it may rather be called a friendly kind of fight than a play or recreation, a bloody and murdering practice than a fellowly sport or pastime."

Puritans and other followers of Calvin took very seriously the biblical commandment, "Remember the sabbath day, to keep it holy" (Exodus 20:8). Sunday was a day of rest from regular work, but it was also the Lord's day. Puritan church services could be very long, with sermons lasting two or three hours. People were expected to spend most of the rest of the day in Bible study and similar activities—definitely not playing football.

DAILY FAITH

Some Reformers were especially concerned with making sure that religion guided every part of people's lives. Jean Calvin thought that government and society should be run according to the Bible. He put this belief into action when the independent city of Geneva, Switzerland, invited him to head the Reformed Church there in 1541. Under his influence, the city council passed laws that regulated almost every aspect of people's behavior. People could be punished for not going to church, for arriving late to church, and for not taking communion often enough. Dancing, card playing, gambling, swearing, and singing irreligious songs were against the law. Women could be put in jail for wearing makeup, elaborate hairstyles, or immodest clothing. Parents were required to give their children biblical names and could not use the names of Catholic saints. Books that disagreed with Reformed teachings were banned. Only religious plays could be performed; eventually even these were outlawed.

Both Catholic and Protestant authorities wanted religion to be a part

Jean Calvin in his study. Calvin was extremely learned and wrote commentaries on almost every book of the Bible.

of everyday life, and for a great many people it was. Even the passage of time (in the days before the wristwatch) was marked by the church. In many towns and villages, both Catholic and Protestant, the day began with church bells ringing to wake people up. In the English countryside, the highest-pitched bell was rung to let harvesters know when it was time to go out to the fields, and again when it was time to leave off work in the evening. In Catholic churches the bells rang at intervals throughout the day to signal the time for various prayers.

Catholics had standard prayers that were recited in Latin, both in and out of church. The most important were the *Pater Noster* ("Our Father," also known as the Lord's Prayer) and the *Ave Maria* ("Hail Mary"). The *Pater Noster* was a prayer that Jesus had taught to his disciples. The *Ave Maria* was based on the words that the angel Gabriel spoke to Mary when he told her that she would be the mother of Jesus. Protestants also used the Lord's Prayer—except it was prayed in the everyday language of the people. Luther translated the prayer into German early on, and other Reformers followed his lead.

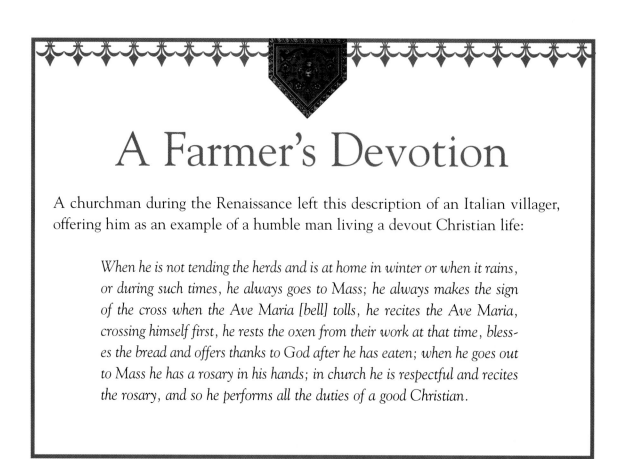

A Farmer's Devotion

A churchman during the Renaissance left this description of an Italian villager, offering him as an example of a humble man living a devout Christian life:

When he is not tending the herds and is at home in winter or when it rains, or during such times, he always goes to Mass; he always makes the sign of the cross when the Ave Maria [bell] tolls, he recites the Ave Maria, crossing himself first, he rests the oxen from their work at that time, blesses the bread and offers thanks to God after he has eaten; when he goes out to Mass he has a rosary in his hands; in church he is respectful and recites the rosary, and so he performs all the duties of a good Christian.

THROUGH THE STAGES OF LIFE

One of the beliefs that Catholics and Protestants shared was the importance of baptism. In this ceremony, a priest or minister welcomed a child into the Christian community by sprinkling it with water (or sometimes briefly dunking it into water) in memory of Jesus' baptism. Because babies during this time period often did not live for very long, baptism was usually performed shortly after birth. Otherwise, according to many people, the soul of an unbaptized child would go to hell. One group of Protestants, however, did not baptize infants or children. Known as Anabaptists, they believed that no one should be baptized until they were an adult and could willingly embrace the Christian faith.

Marriage was one of the stages of life that both Catholics and Protestants celebrated in church. In this Catholic wedding ceremony, the priest is blessing the bride and groom's union.

Childhood experiences varied according to a number of factors. Most Renaissance children received little education because they had to help their parents work. A Catholic child from a well-off family might be sent to school in a monastery. Public schools were beginning to appear in greater number, especially in cities. However, most of them charged fees that few families could afford. Calvin's Geneva looked to the future by requiring that all children go to school. Well-to-do parents were expected to contribute to the costs of running the schools, but poor children could attend for free. The students, both girls and boys, learned reading, writing, arithmetic, and religion. For many years, though, there was no public secondary school for girls to attend—usually, only boys were able to continue their formal education.

Many boys, and a small number of girls, became apprentices to learn a craft or trade. In this area, too, religion could play a role. In Catholic communities, each craft and trade had its own patron saint. The craftspeople would celebrate this saint's feast day and might attend a church dedicated to the saint. As the Reformation took hold, it became common for apprentices to have to meet religious requirements. For example, in Nuremburg after 1525, only Lutherans were allowed to become apprentices.

As we have seen, Catholic and Protestant ideas about marriage were the same in some ways and different in others. Two things that almost everyone agreed on was that engagements should be publicly announced and that wedding ceremonies should be held in church. This had not always been the case in the past. The sixteenth century also saw an increasing emphasis on the bride and groom promising to love and care for each other. The Church of England's *Book of Common Prayer* put this promise into words that are still heard at numerous weddings today: "I . . . take thee . . . to have and to hold from this day forward, for better, for worse, for richer, for poorer, in sickness and in health, to love and to cherish, till death us depart, according to God's holy ordinance: and thereto I plight thee my troth."

Seven

LEARNING TOLERANCE

I n 1555, the Holy Roman Emperor signed a treaty that granted German princes and dukes the right to decide whether their territories would be Catholic or Lutheran. Almost everywhere, in fact, it was European rulers who ultimately decided what people's religion would be. Separation between church and state was almost completely unknown. If a ruler became Protestant, he made Protestantism the state religion. Every Christian in the country was generally expected to follow the same religious path.

MARTYRS ON BOTH SIDES

Whether in a Catholic or Protestant country, anyone in a religious minority could have a difficult time. Part of this was a result of the government's involvement with religion. Most rulers and independent city governments believed that a population that was split between different churches could not be effectively governed. The general opinion was that religious unity was necessary for national strength.

Many Protestant countries regarded the pope as a foreign power. Catholics were therefore easily suspected of treason because of their acceptance of the pope's authority. The suspicion was strengthened when Catholic subjects did, sometimes, plot rebellions against Protestant rulers, as in England during the reign of Queen Elizabeth.

England between Two Religions

In most of Europe, once a ruler decided to either remain Catholic or switch to Protestantism, the country's official religion did not change afterward. England, however, was a different case. When Henry VIII established the Church of England in 1534, he accepted nearly all Catholic beliefs except the authority of the pope. (He did, however, close all of England's monasteries and take over their property and income.) During his reign, Protestants who rejected other important Catholic teachings were punished as heretics—people who rejected and endangered religious truth—and treated as harshly as Catholics who remained loyal to the pope. Henry's son, Edward VI, on the other hand, was a much more dedicated Protestant. During his short reign (1547–1553) English replaced Latin as the language for worship services, images of saints were destroyed or removed from churches, and priests were allowed to marry. Many Catholics were put in prison, and two were executed for heresy.

When Edward's half-sister Mary Tudor took the throne, the nation's religion changed once again, for Mary was an ardent Catholic. When she first became queen, she declared that she would not force her subjects to follow religious beliefs that were against their conscience. Instead, she hoped that Protestants could be convinced to convert to Catholicism by

*Sir Thomas More, England's great humanist writer, was one of many
Renaissance people who were killed because of their religious beliefs. The
Catholic Church declared More a saint in 1935.*

peaceful and reasonable means. In 1555, however, Mary began to allow the
persecution of Protestants, and soon she encouraged it. Three hundred or
so Protestants were executed during her reign. These martyrdoms strengthened the faith and determination of Protestants, and made many Catholics
ashamed of the violence that was done in the name of their church.

In 1558 Mary died and her half-sister Elizabeth, a Protestant, became England's ruler. One of her first actions as queen was to forge a compromise between Protestantism and Catholicism. She again made English the language of worship, authorized the publication of an English Bible, and permitted priests to marry. At the same time, she kept some of the Catholic Church's ceremonies, required priests to wear special robes (like Catholic priests, but unlike ministers in many Protestant groups), and supported traditional-style church music. All English citizens had to attend Church of England services, but there was tolerance for people's private religious beliefs.

Most of the people were happy with Elizabeth's compromise, but the country's religious problems still weren't over. In 1570 the pope excommunicated Elizabeth and gave Catholic rulers of other countries permission to overthrow her. In the early 1580s a group of Catholic nobles plotted against Elizabeth, and the Spanish ambassador was involved in a conspiracy to depose her. These and similar events made Elizabeth's government so suspicious of Catholics that in 1585 all Catholic priests were banished from England.

Then Spain declared war, with the pope's blessing, and partly for the purpose of making England a Catholic country again. Jesuit missionaries who had come to England to try to convert people to Catholicism were regarded as spies for the pope or for Spain. They were treated severely whenever they were caught. One Jesuit described the scene in England following the defeat of the Spanish Armada in 1588, after fears of a Spanish invasion were quelled: "The Spanish Fleet had exasperated the people against the Catholics . . . everywhere a hunt was being organized for Catholics and their houses searched." Even Elizabeth, one of Europe's most able rulers, could not fully overcome the religious intolerance of her age.

The problem was that both sides were sure that they were absolutely right—their form of Christianity was the only true faith. Anything that differed was seen as a threat, and anyone on the "wrong" side was doomed to eternal suffering in hell. Catholics branded Protestants as heretics, and Protestants did the same to Catholics. In addition, mainstream Protestants joined with Catholics in condemning Anabaptists and other "radical" Protestant sects. The Catholic Church and many Protestant authorities agreed that heretics were enemies of God and deserved the worst possible punishment. This punishment was frequently public execution by burning.

Inquisitions

Since the 1200s the Church had had a special court to find, try, and punish heretics. It was called the Inquisition. By the 1400s it was not very active, except in Spain. There, the Spanish Inquisition pursued not only Christian heretics but also converts to Christianity who were suspected of returning to their original Muslim or Jewish practices. From 1483 to 1498 alone, the Spanish Inquisition executed more than two thousand people. After the Reformation, it persecuted Protestants as well. The Spanish Inquisition also operated in regions ruled by Spain, especially the Low Countries (modern Netherlands and Belgium). Antwerp was the first Low Countries city to have Protestant martyrs when two monks who had accepted Luther's teachings were burned at the stake in 1523. By 1546, roughly one thousand Anabaptists had been executed in the Low Countries.

In 1542 the Catholic Church reorganized the Inquisition to combat Protestantism in Italy. Before long there were few Protestants left on the peninsula—most of those who had not been arrested fled for their lives, settling in Switzerland or Germany. In 1549 King Henry II of France set up his own special commission to hunt down and prosecute heretics. Sixty Protestants were burned within three years. As in other inquisitions at this

Both Catholic and Protestant leaders tried to control the ideas that their people could read about. Both sides burned books that were thought to threaten the religious or political order.

time, anyone who owned books or pamphlets written by Luther or other Reformers was suspect. It was illegal to print, sell, or possess these written materials, and they were destroyed when they were found. The burning of banned books was a common practice among both Catholics and Protestants.

In places where Reformers gained government control, they could be almost as ruthless as the Inquisition. Sir Thomas More, the great writer and statesman, was beheaded in 1535 for rejecting Henry VIII's authority over the church in England. Many of Luther's followers urged German governments to give the death penalty to people who practiced "false religion." Geneva burned its first heretic in 1553. In the 1570s Calvinists temporarily gained control of many places in the Low Countries. Their violence against Catholics prompted a poet in Amsterdam to write, "They who at first asked for no more than to live in freedom, / Now have their liberty, but will not give it to others."

LOOKING FORWARD

The sixteenth century's various forms of Christianity gave many people the spiritual guidance and certainty that they longed for. But the religious conflict also created widespread suffering. From 1546 to 1555, Holy Roman Emperor Charles V and the Catholic rulers of German territories warred against German Protestant rulers. In 1560 France entered into thirty-eight years of civil war, with Catholics and Protestants fighting one another all over the country. The worst episode during these Wars of Religion was the Saint Bartholomew's Day Massacre, which began on August 24, 1572. Catholic mobs attacked and killed Protestants, known as Huguenots, in the streets of Paris. The violence spread to the countryside and to other cities and lasted almost a week. Thousands of Huguenots died. In 1598 the battles and riots finally died down when the Edict of Nantes granted religious freedom to Protestants.

Like many people witnessing the events of the French Wars of Religion, Michel de Montaigne was filled with dismay by the violence around him. He saw that the wars were "the true school of . . . inhumanity." Montaigne, a retired civil servant from a noble family, found comfort in the activity of writing. He invented a new literary form, the personal essay, which he used for self-examination. He felt that "all the evils of this world are engendered by those who teach us not to be aware of our own ignorance." Through self-awareness, according to Montaigne, a person would increase in tolerance and good sense, and would not give way to extreme behaviors. In other words, once you realize that you don't know everything, you are much less likely to be judgmental or cruel to others.

A Third Way

Some years before Montaigne, the great scholar Erasmus had also written in favor of tolerance. Erasmus was able to see both sides of the debate between Protestants and Catholics. He personally preferred a simple form of Christianity, yet he remained loyal to the Catholic Church. He could not join Luther in rejecting the Church's teachings about the importance of good works and of human beings having free will to choose good or evil. Erasmus nevertheless hoped that the Church could be purified of corruption and thought that it shouldn't be necessary to choose between Catholicism and Protestantism. He believed there was a third way, a way of communication instead of conflict. The Catholic Church, he said, could be reformed gradually, from the inside.

For Erasmus and his followers, the key to reforming both Church and society was knowledge. The better educated people were, the better they would be able to recognize and understand religious truth. Truth, Erasmus believed, would always win out in any reasonable discussion among knowledgeable people. It made much more sense, meanwhile, to accept dif-

One of Erasmus's most famous works, The Praise of Folly, *poked fun at many human failings. Yet, though Erasmus never ignored these shortcomings, he remained convinced that if people had access to knowledge, they would always choose to do good.*

ferences of opinion on religion than to use violence or other extreme measures to try to force everyone to agree to the same set of beliefs.

Throughout the sixteenth century, Erasmus and Montaigne were joined by a few other voices speaking for tolerance and true religious freedom. Among these voices were some of the Anabaptists. Because of the persecution they endured from government-supported churches on both sides, Anabaptists became strong advocates of separating church and state. During the 1600s, this idea would be taken up by more and more people, including the founders of the American colonies of Rhode Island and Pennsylvania. In the 1700s, separation of church and state was championed by the likes of Thomas Jefferson and James Madison.

The success of the American Revolution brought about a true revolution in society and government's attitude toward matters of faith. As the new United States took shape, James Madison spearheaded the creation of the Bill of Rights, ten amendments to the Constitution that would guarantee Americans' personal liberty. The very first statement in the First Amendment is, "Congress shall make no law respecting an establishment of religion, or prohibiting the free exercise thereof." This affirmation of people's most basic right, to decide for themselves how to relate (or not relate) to the divine, at last held out the promise of real religious freedom. The struggles of the sixteenth century remind us how precious this freedom truly is.

GLOSSARY

Anabaptists "radical" Protestants who believed that only adults, not babies, should be baptized. Many Anabaptists also supported nonviolence and gave women and men equal roles in religion.

apprentice a young person being trained in a craft or trade by assisting and working for a master in that craft or trade

bishop a high-ranking priest in the Catholic Church or Church of England who oversees religious affairs for a particular region

Catholic refers to the branch of Christianity under the authority of the pope

congregation the group of people who attend a particular church

convent common term for a women's monastery

dowry money, property, and goods supplied by a bride's family for her to bring into her marriage

excommunication action taken by the Catholic Church to deny Holy Communion and the other sacraments to a person or group of people, usually as a punishment for a serious crime against Church law; the exclusion of a person from Church membership

fresco a wall painting made on fresh plaster

Holy Roman Empire an empire made up primarily of German, Austrian, and Italian territories, founded in 962 with the idea of unifying Europe

Huguenots French Protestants, followers of Jean (John) Calvin

humanism an approach to learning that emphasized study of the subjects known as the humanities: grammar, rhetoric, literature, philosophy, and history. A **humanist** was someone who had thoroughly studied the humanities.

martyr someone who is killed because of their religion

missionary a person who travels to a far-off place to teach his or her religion to the people of that place

monastery a religious institution where monks or nuns live apart from the world, devoting themselves to prayer and study

monk a man who lives in a monastery, taking lifelong vows of poverty, chastity, and obedience

Muslim a follower of Islam, the religion founded in seventh-century Arabia by Muhammad

nun a woman who lives in a convent, taking lifelong vows of poverty, chastity, and obedience

Ottoman Empire an empire based in Turkey, founded in the fourteenth century. At its peak in the 1500s it included North Africa, most of the Middle East, and much of southeastern Europe.

patron someone who gives financial support and other encouragement to an artist, musician, writer, etc.

penance actions undertaken to atone for, or make up for, sins

pilgrimage a journey to a holy site, such as a place associated with Jesus or a church with important saints' relics

Protestant refers to Christians who reject the authority of the pope and many practices and beliefs of the Catholic Church

Puritans English Protestants who followed the teachings of Jean Calvin

Reformation the movement begun in 1517 by Martin Luther to reform the Catholic Church. Eventually the Reformation resulted in the founding of many different kinds of Christian groups, such as Lutherans, Anglicans (Episcopalians), Calvinists (Presbyterians), and Baptists.

Roman Empire At its height, the empire stretched from Spain to the Middle East, reaching north to include what is now England and south to include North Africa. In 330 the empire's capital moved from Rome to Constantinople, and in 364 the empire was divided into eastern and western halves. The last emperor of the Western Empire was overthrown in 476, while the Eastern Empire survived, as the Byzantine Empire, for nearly a thousand years more.

rosary a string of beads, held in the hands, used by many Catholics to assist in their praying

saint a person recognized by the Catholic Church as being especially holy and able to perform miracles both during life and after death

FOR FURTHER READING

Ashby, Ruth. *Elizabethan England*. New York: Benchmark Books, 1999.

Greenblatt, Miriam. *Elizabeth I and Tudor England*. New York: Benchmark Books, 2002.

Greenblatt, Miriam. *Lorenzo de' Medici and Renaissance Italy*. New York: Benchmark Books, 2003.

Halliwell, Sarah, editor. *The Renaissance: Artists and Writers*. Austin: Raintree Steck-Vaughn, 1998.

Hinds, Kathryn. *Venice and Its Merchant Empire*. New York: Benchmark Books, 2001.

Howarth, Sarah. *Renaissance People*. Brookfield, CT: Millbrook Press, 1992.

Howarth, Sarah. *Renaissance Places*. Brookfield, CT: Millbrook Press, 1992.

Mann, Kenny. *Isabel, Ferdinand, and Fifteenth-Century Spain*. New York: Benchmark Books, 2001.

Matthews, Rupert. *The Renaissance*. New York: Peter Bedrick, 2000.

Merlo, Claudio. *Three Masters of the Renaissance: Leonardo, Michelangelo, Raphael*. Translated by Marion Lignana Rosenberg. Hauppauge, NY: Barron's Educational Series, 1999.

Millar, Heather. *Spain in the Age of Exploration*. New York: Benchmark Books, 1999.

Mühlberger, Richard. *What Makes a Leonardo a Leonardo?* New York: The Metropolitan Museum of Art/Viking, 1994.

Netzley, Patricia D. *Life During the Renaissance*. San Diego: Lucent Books, 1998.

Pollard, Michael. *Johann Gutenberg, Master of Modern Printing*. Woodbridge, CT: Blackbirch Press, 2001.

Schomp, Virginia. *The Italian Renaissance*. New York: Benchmark Books, 2003.

Thomas, Jane Resh. *Behind the Mask: The Life of Queen Elizabeth I*. New York: Clarion Books, 1998.

Ventura, Piero. *Michelangelo's World*. New York: Putnam, 1989.

ON-LINE INFORMATION*

Annenberg/CPB. *Renaissance*.
　　http://www.learner.org/exhibits/renaissance
The Artchive: Renaissance Art.
　　http://artchive.com/artchive/renaissance.html
Johnson, Phillip R. *The Hall of Church History: The Reformers*.
　　http://www.gty.org/~phil/reformers.htm
Kren, Emil, and Daniel Marx. *Web Gallery of Art: Guided Tours*.
　　http://gallery.euroweb.hu/tours/index.html
Matthews, Kevin. *Renaissance Architecture*.
　　http://www.greatbuildings.com/types/styles/renaissance.html
Renaissance.
　　http://renaissance.dm.net
Vatican Exhibit.
　　http://www.ibiblio.org/expo/vatican.exhibit/Vatican.exhibit.html

*Websites change from time to time. For additional on-line information, check with the media specialist at your local library.

BIBLIOGRAPHY

Black, C. F., et al. *Cultural Atlas of the Renaissance*. New York: Prentice Hall General Reference, 1993.

Davis, Natalie Zemon. *Society and Culture in Early Modern France*. Stanford, CA: University of Stanford Press, 1975.

Douglass, Jane Dempsey. "Women and the Continental Reformation" in *Religion and Sexism: Images of Woman in the Jewish and Christian Traditions*, edited by Rosemary Radford Ruether, pp. 292–318. New York: Simon and Schuster, 1974.

Durant, Will. *The Reformation: A History of European Civilization from Wyclif to Calvin: 1300–1564 (The Story of Civilization, vol. VI)*. New York: Simon and Schuster, 1957.

Editors of Time-Life Books. *What Life Was Like in the Realm of Elizabeth: England AD 1533–1603*. Alexandria, VA: Time-Life Books, 1998.

Ferguson, Sinclair B., and David F. Wright, editors. *New Dictionary of Theology*. Downers Grove, IL: InterVarsity Press, 1988.

Ginzburg, Carlo. *The Night Battles: Witchcraft and Agrarian Cults in the Sixteenth and Seventeenth Centuries*. Translated by John and Anne Tedeschi. New York: Penguin Books, 1985.

Hale, John. *The Civilization of Europe in the Renaissance*. New York: Touchstone, 1993.

Hoffmeister, Gerhart, editor. *The Renaissance and Reformation in Germany: An Introduction*. New York: Frederick Ungar Publishing, 1977.

Johnson, Paul. *The Renaissance: A Short History*. New York: Modern Library, 2000.

Kekewich, Lucille, editor. *The Impact of Humanism*. New Haven and London: Yale University Press, 2000.

King, Margaret L. *Women of the Renaissance*. Chicago and London: University of Chicago Press, 1991.

Liebowitz, Ruth P. "Virgins in the Service of Christ: The Dispute over an Active Apostolate for Women during the Counter-Reformation" in *Women of Spirit: Female Leadership in the Jewish and Christian Traditions*, edited by Rosemary Ruether and Eleanor McLaughlin, pp. 131–152. New York: Simon and Schuster, 1979.

Logan, George M., et al., editors. *The Norton Anthology of English Literature, Seventh Edition, Volume 1B: The Sixteenth Century, the Early Seventeenth Century*. New York: Norton, 2000.

Mottola, Anthony, translator. *The Spiritual Exercises of St. Ignatius*. Introduction by Robert W. Gleason. Garden City, NY: Image Books, 1964.

Metford, J. C. J. *Dictionary of Christian Lore and Legend*. London: Thames and Hudson, 1983.

Mitchell, Bonner. *Rome in the High Renaissance: The Age of Leo X*. Norman, OK: University of Oklahoma Press, 1973.

Murray, John J. *Antwerp in the Age of Plantin and Brueghel*. Norman, OK: University of Oklahoma Press, 1970.

Pritchard, R. E., editor. *Shakespeare's England: Life in Elizabethan and Jacobean Times*. Gloucestershire: Sutton Publishing, 1999.

Rabb, Theodore. *Renaissance Lives: Portraits of an Age*. New York: Pantheon, 1993.

Rowse, A. L. *The Elizabethan Renaissance: The Life of the Society*. New York: Charles Scribner's Sons, 1971.

Shakespeare, William. *Complete Works, Compact Edition*. Edited by Stanley Wells et al. Oxford: Clarendon Press, 1988.

Strauss, Gerald. *Nuremberg in the Sixteenth Century*. New York: John Wiley, 1966.

INDEX

Page numbers for illustrations are in boldface

Alexander VI, Pope, 27, 48
America, religious freedom
    in, 84–85
Anabaptists, 74, 81, 85
apprentices, 76
archbishops, 24, 31, 48
artists, Renaissance, 26, 27,
    39
Augustinian Order, 50

baptism, **22**, 23, 32, 74
Benedict, Saint, 49, 50
Bible, New Testament, 13,
    14, 32, 33, 35, 64
bishops, 24, 30, 48, 57
books, **8**, **9**, 83
Borgia, Cesare, 27, 48
Borgia, Lucrezia, 27
Bridget of Ireland, Saint, 20

Calvin, Jean, 37, 42, 45, 71,
    72, **73**, 76
Calvinists, 44, 71, 72, 83
cardinals, 25–26, 27, **27**,
    30
Catholicism, 9, 10, 12, 28,
    29, 36, 37, 38, **56**
    acts of grace, 21, **22**, 23
    Catholic churches,
        41–43, **43**
    clergymen, 46, **47**,
        48–51, **49**, **51**
    community life, 38, **39**,
        40–45, **40**, **43**, **45**

daily faith, 72–73
holy days, 68–72, **69**
holy orders, 23, 48, 61
the Inquisition, 81, 83
popes, 24–27, **25**, **26**,
    30–32, **31**, 78
Protestantism vs., 77–81
saints, 16, **17**, 20–21,
    20, 49, 50, 53, **53**,
    62–63, **63**
women and, 40, 55, **56**,
    57–60, **59**, 62–63, **63**

Charles V, Holy Roman
    Emperor, 33, 77, 83
children, 76
Christianity, 10, **11**, 12,
    28–29
    the Church's growth, 16,
        17, 20–21, **20**
    story of Jesus, **11**, 13–14,
        13, **15**
Christopher, Saint, 20, **20**,
    21
Church of England, 37, 54,
    76, 78, 80
College of Cardinals, 25–26
Columbus, Christopher, 9
Communion, Holy, 21, 23,
    32, 37, 42, 71
Company of Saint Ursula,
    62
Constantine, 16, 34
convents, 57, 60, 62, 63

daily faith, 72–73
dark ages, 7
Discalced Carmelites, 63
disciples, 14, 20
Dominic, Saint, **39**
Dominican Order, 39, 50–51
Donation of Constantine,
    34–35

Eastern Orthodox Church,
    28
Edict of Nantes, 83
education, 76
Edward VI (England), 78
Elizabeth I, 71, 78, 80
England
    between two religions,
        78–81
    Church of England, 37,
        54, 76, 78, 80
Erasmus, 35, 44, 84–85, **85**
excommunication, 26, 33,
    80

Florence, Italy, 7, 26, 68
Fra Angelico, 39, 40
Francis of Assisi, Saint, 62
Franciscan Order, 51
French Wars of Religion, 84
Fust, Johann, 9

Gabriel, angel, **40**
government and religion,
    77–81, **82**, 83, 85–86

Gutenberg, Johannes, 9

Henry II (France), 81
Henry VIII (England), 37,
    41, 78, 83
heretics, 81, 83
holy days, 68–72, **69**
Holy Roman Empire, 32,
    33, 67
Huguenots, 83
humanism, 34–35, **35**, 44

indulgences, 30–32, **31**
Inquisition, the, 81, 83

Jefferson, Thomas, 85
Jesuits, 51, 80
Jesus, **11**, 13–14, **13**, **15**,
    16, 21, **22**, 24, 63, 68
Jews, 13, 14, 16, 28–29, **29**
John the Baptist, 14, **15**, **22**
Joseph, 14, 20, 21
Judaism, 16
Judea, 13–14
Julius II, Pope, 26, **26**

Leo X, Pope, 30, 31, 32
Loyola, Ignatius, 51, 52–53,
    53
Luther, Martin, 9, 31–33,
    33, 35, 36, 37, 45, 50,
    54, 61, 64, 73
Lutheranism, 37

Madison, James, 85
marriage, 23, 48, 57, 61, 64,
    75, 76
martyrs, Christian, 20, 79,
    79, 81, 83
Mary Magdalene, **11**
Mary, mother of Jesus, **13**,
    14, **15**, 20, **40**, 69, 71
Mary Tudor, 78–80

Medici, Lorenzo de', 26
Merici, Angela, 62
Michelangelo, 27
Middle Ages, 26
ministers, protestant, 54
monasteries, 37, 38, 40–41,
    40, 49, 57, 58, 60,
    62–63
monks, 40, 49–51, **49**, **51**,
    57, 81
Montaigne, Michel de, 84,
    85
More, Sir Thomas, **79**, 83
Muslims, 13, 28, 52

Ninty-five Theses, 32
nuns, 40, 55, 57–60, **59**,
    62–63, **63**

Ottoman Empire, 28

Papal States, 26
parish church, 41–42
parishes, 24, 48
pastors, 54, 65
Patrick, Saint, 21
patrons, 21
Paul III, Pope, 53
Peter, Saint, 24
Petrarch, 7
plague, 10, 12
popes, 24–27, **25**, **26**,
    30–32, **31**, 78
prayers, 73, 76
predestination, 36
priests, 23, 30, **43**, 46, 48,
    54, 57, 64, 65, 80
printing press, invention of,
    9
Protestant Reformation, 9,
    12, 32–33, **33**, 36–37,
    51
    nuns and the, 60

Protestantism, 12, 38, 41,
    42
    Catholicism vs., 77–81
    daily faith, 72–73
    holy days, 68–72, **69**
    Inquisitions against, 81,
        83
    Protestant churches,
        41–42, 43–45, **45**
    Protestant ministers, 54
    women serving God in
        the home, 61, **61**,
        64–66
Puritans, 37, 72

Raphael, 26, 27
relics, holy, 21
religious freedom, 84–85
Renaissance, the, 7, **8**, 9
Roman Empire, 10, 14, 16,
    34
Rule of Saint Benedict, 49,
    50

Saint Bartholomew's Day
    Massacre, 83
Saint Peter's basilica, 27, 31
saints, 16, **17**, 20–21, **20**, 49,
    50, 53, **53**, 62–63, **63**
separation of church and
    state, 77, 85
seven sacraments, 21, **22**,
    23, 26
Shakespeare, William,
    18–19, **18**
Sixtus IV, Pope, **25**
Society of Jesus, 51, 52–53
Spanish Armada, 80
Spanish Inquisition, 81

Tarabotti, Arcangela, 58–59
Teresa of Avila, Saint, 62,
    63, **63**

tolerance, religious, 84–85
Trinity, 13, 23, 42

Ursulines, 62

Valla, Lorenzo, 34–35

Wars of Religion, 83–84
women and the Church, **56**
    during holy days, 71
    nuns, 40, 55, 57–60, **59**,
        62–63, **63**
    religious societies,
        62–63, **63**

serving God in the
    home, 61, **61**, 64–66
witch hunts, 66–67, **67**

Zell, Katherine, 65
Zwingli, Ulrich, 36–37